WE NEED TO TALK ABOUT PARENTS

In Loving Memory of Margaret Knowles

WE NEED TO TALK ABOUT PARENTS

A TEACHERS' GUIDE TO WORKING WITH FAMILIES

CATHIE FREEMAN AND JENNI GATES

SAGE Publications Ltd
1 Oliver's Yard
55 City Road
London EC1Y 1SP

CORWIN
A SAGE company
2455 Teller Road
Thousand Oaks, California 91320
(0800)233-9936
www.corwin.com

SAGE Publications India Pvt Ltd
B 1/I 1 Mohan Cooperative Industrial Area
Mathura Road
New Delhi 110 044

SAGE Publications Asia-Pacific Pte Ltd
3 Church Street
#10-04 Samsung Hub
Singapore 049483

Editor: James Clark
Senior assistant editor: Diana Alves
Production editor: Katherine Haw
Copyeditor: Bryan Campbell
Proofreader: Christine Bitten
Indexer: Adam Pozner
Marketing manager: Dilhara Attygalle
Cover design: Wendy Scott
Typeset by: KnowledgeWorks Global Ltd.
Printed in the UK

Library of Congress Control Number: 2021947108

British Library Cataloguing in Publication data

A catalogue record for this book is available from the British Library

ISBN 978-1-5297-5167-3
ISBN 978-1-5297-5166-6 (pbk)

At SAGE we take sustainability seriously. Most of our products are printed in the UK using responsibly sourced papers and boards. When we print overseas we ensure sustainable papers are used as measured by the PREPS grading system. We undertake an annual audit to monitor our sustainability.

CONTENTS

ABOUT THE AUTHORS

Cathie Freeman currently works within a talking therapy service for the NHS as a senior psychological wellbeing practitioner, and has worked within mental health since graduating as an Occupational Therapist. As the spouse of a serving Royal Marine, Cathie spent a lot of her adult life moving within the UK, as well as the USA where she worked as a substitute teacher within the local school. Cathie cares passionately about psychological wellbeing and believes it to be a fundamental aspect to realise and live our full potential.

Jenni Gates is currently working in private practice as an integrative counselling therapist in Devon, UK, as well as offering online counselling internationally. Jenni has many years of experience working with young people and families in schools and education settings, across the UK, with a focus on mental health and wellbeing; she believes education is key to a happier and healthier world.

www.jennigatestherapy.co.uk

ACKNOWLEDGEMENTS

There are many people that Cathie and Jenni would like to thank, in making this book possible. First of all, their fabulous editors: Diana Alves, who has worked tirelessly and patiently in guiding and supporting the authors chapter by chapter, along with James Clark, both of SAGE Publications. The authors would also like to give special thanks to Scott Buckler, Ally Strang-Faulds, Alice Tolman-May and Pooky Knightsmith, for their support, advice, and teaching expertise that has undoubtedly enriched this resource.

Cathie would like to thank all the teachers who have personally inspired her, enabling her to find her passion – which is the foundation for all this book brings to life. She would like to thank co-author, Jenni, for her mentorship, knowledge and expertise throughout this process, but mostly her deeply valued friendship. With heartfelt gratitude, Cathie would like to thank her loving parents, Margaret and George for their lifelong love and support. She would like to express her wholehearted appreciation to her husband Ian, for his unwavering support and continued encouragement and finally, her two children, Jasmine and Nicole, who have been Cathie's most profound educators and inspiration.

Jenni would like to give a special shout-out to her dear friend and co-author Cathie. Cathie has led the way with this book, and has done so skillfully, passionately, and admirably, through the most challenging times, in which this book was written. Jenni has thoroughly enjoyed collaborating with Cathie and all she has learnt in this process. And last, but not least, Jenni would like to thank Bill and their children Finlay and Annabel for their love, support and encouragement. Writing books, whilst full-time working can involve some antisocial working hours, and Cathie and Jenni both very much appreciate their supportive families making this book possible.

ABOUT THE WEBSITE

On the address **www.values2connection.co.uk** you shall find supporting materials for this book, including extended resources, further reading lists, and some templates for use with families, that are free for you to download.

INTRODUCTION

We need to talk about parents because working with families is a fundamental part of teaching. Each child in every classroom has a backstory of their own; they have caregivers whom they spend the other part of their life with. Children develop in response to their environment – of school, home and community, so it makes sense that we should look at the raising, education and nurturing of children in a collaborative way. There are endless resources on parenting and teaching but little in the way of working together. This book offers a structured approach to enhancing those relationships from the teacher's perspective; working from the inside out. This approach is necessary to maintain and build relationships successfully.

What does that mean in practical terms? It means developing meaningful connections beyond the classroom. There are many ways to build these connections, and many things that inhibit the development and maintenance of the relationships, that is what this book directly addresses in the context of the teacher, family and wider community. By starting with the teacher and working from the inside out, we aim to empower authenticity and self-awareness within the student and their parent(s) through facilitating effective engagement between the teacher and the school. The societal interplay between the teacher, school and family can demand many additional resources beyond those the teacher is initially equipped with, in facilitating learning, derived through their training. However, the Department for Education published on www.gov.uk on the 10th March 2018, that 22.5% of teachers leave the profession within two years, 32.3% leaving in under five years, often citing additional pressures such as working with parents, alongside the continued increase in child and adolescent emotional and mental health issues (DfE, 2018). We believe this book has never been more needed.

There are many (sometimes unspoken) interpersonal situations that a teacher is required to respond to in the classroom such as loss, difficulties at home, abuse, low self-esteem, special educational needs and so on. Alongside the child bringing these issues to school, so do the teachers, parents, families and wider school community. This can often take up a great deal of time, although a necessary and needed part of the job. Left unmanaged it can add unmeasurable amounts of stress on the teacher. This is not something that is addressed within teacher training, but we are here to help. As authors, we are mental health professionals with experience of working with young people and families in a variety of settings, including schools and education centres across the UK as well as in the USA. We offer a supportive gateway to communication and connection, from the perspective of the teacher. In doing so we take care to prioritise teacher wellbeing and psychological safety, as we talk you through each stage of our values based connection model, with the understanding of the extremely demanding nature of your role.

Whilst the book will provide strategies from professional academic fields (such as those evolving within education, psychology, counselling and therapy), it also provides a framework for successful development of a holistic approach that benefits the full school community, by working from the perspective of the teacher to cultivate authenticity and optimise communication. Such a framework is rare, and whilst initiatives such as 'Thrive' have become prevalent in schools, there is questionable worth of the Thrive approach, due to the lack of theoretical structure and counselling skills required for those delivering such packages, resulting in a loose collection of techniques from psychotherapy that risks causing more harm than good, used within the classroom context. This book offers enhanced personal development to aid the teacher in managing difficult communications with parents, and the generalised stressors that come with modern teaching. This unique aim shall encompass strategies and advice for the teacher and the wider school community in order to help the child flourish.

Education is the lighting of a fire and the most effective way of lighting a fire is directly from our own flame. That is why this book works from the inside out: working from the values and passion of the teacher to ignite the flames within their students. By development and discussion of fundamental ideas which enhance psychological wellbeing and advance interpersonal skills, we aim to not only benefit teachers personally but also enhance collaboration with families and the wider school community. Working together we can all keep those fires burning, empowering children to use their gifts benefiting all of society. If we can keep your flame burning, support you, and work with you to continue to be the beating heart of the community, we can also enable our youngsters to thrive.

We are all cogs in a much bigger machine when it comes to young minds; however, we can only focus on our own influence and responsibilities, and seek to understand ourselves in order to bring the best version of ourselves to all we do. As teachers are direct influencers of the developing child, we focus on supporting you to model a way of being which communicates a much more powerful message, to all that we interact with. This is a practical guide, illustrated with fabricated scenarios, to bring concepts to life, which we hope will enhance parent teacher relationships, through the development of sustainable personal and professional growth. By connecting well with yourself it is much easier to connect with others. Education derives from the latin *educere*, which translates to 'lead out'; nothing leads out more effectively than modelling and leading by example.

References

DfE (2018) *Factors affecting teacher retention: qualitative investigation.* Available at: https://assets.publishing.service.gov.uk/government/uploads/system/uploads/attachment_data/file/686947/Factors_affecting_teacher_retention_-_qualitative_investigation.pdf (accessed 9 August 2021).

1

VALUES

──────────────── Chapter objectives ────────────────

- What are values and why do they matter?
- To explore values, beliefs and behaviours
- What are the types of values and how do they impact on relationships?
- How do we develop rules based on values?
- To consider freedom of speech and fundamental values
- To examine how to manage conflicting values and beliefs
- To understand how to develop a value-based community and apply this to your school.

Introduction

It took great deliberation to find the right starting point for this book, because the topic of working with families is broad, and there are so many different relational qualities and interplay of dynamics between teacher, pupil, class, school, parent, family and the wider community to consider. So, we decided to structure this book to reflect our values based connection model of working with families, beginning with the inner core. You shall be aware of overlap and interconnections that weave through the book, and you may wish to refer back to Figure 1.1 as you go.

Our aim is to work from the inside out. That is, first of all, inviting you (the reader) as an individual to self-reflect in order that we can then consider wider perspectives and how we engage as relational beings in our classroom, beyond, and more specifically, with parents.

In modern education, there are great demands on the teacher, and many lines of authority that dictate the day-to-day running of a classroom, as well as what is taught

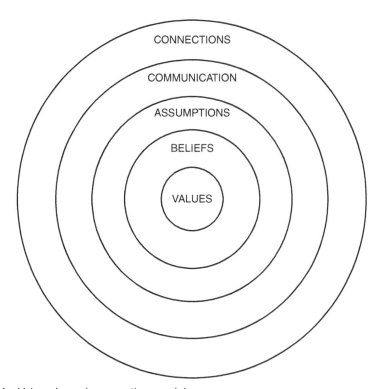

Figure 1.1 Values based connection model

and how we teach it. There is often little emphasis on the wellbeing and needs of the teacher, and pupil/family welfare takes precedence above all. We want to change that. You are super important, and your unique being and all that you bring to your profession as an individual, should be honoured and cherished. We all know about the importance of self-care, and the necessity of looking after ourselves before we can effectively care for others, but in reality our various professional and personal roles can make putting this into practice far more difficult. This book is here, putting you at the centre, and as an outcome, it shall enhance your interpersonal relationships, both professionally and socially. And so, our starting place is here – and considering *you* the person, before *you* the teacher.

About you

At the beginning of a new term, or on our first meeting with a student, we very often build relationships by asking the student to share something about themselves. A student might tell of their favourite sports team, who they live with and if they have any pets at home, what they enjoy doing in their free time, and so on. Normally a student will share something that is of value to them, and typically the student will not offer an explanation for why the facts about them that they chose to share are significant enough for them to do so. The information the student gives us, helps us gain access to learn a little more about that person, but we need more information than this to really understand anything of that individual's core being. In our first encounter/lesson with the same student, we might notice the way in which they socially interact with others in the classroom. Is the student confident in contributing to class discussion? Does the student like to ask or answer questions? What clues does the student's body language give about them? Perhaps we also have information that has been handed over from previous teachers, or from the school about the levels the student works at. These are some of the initial sources of information that we use to form our first impressions of our student. However, this information does not help us understand the value system of any individual and the things that are truly important to them. So, are we asking the right questions?

Now let's try this out for ourselves.

Exercise 1.1

Know thyself (*Nosce te ipsum*)

1 How do you describe yourself and why? Try writing a brief personal state-ment starting 'My name is...'. How you describe yourself can often be dependent on context, but it is interesting to analyse why we select the identity labels that we do, for what purpose, and what do we want to com-municate about ourselves (or not) to the person requesting the information?

2 Now try writing a statement starting 'The most Important things to me in the world are...'. Once complete, can you look back to your first statement and consider if any of your values are conveyed initially?

3 Next, write a list of your core values and associated beliefs.

4 Finally, how do your values align with those of the school in which you work?

Table 1.1 Values and intent

Value	Belief	What intentions	What behaviour
Integrity	I believe you should always be honest.	I will always tell the truth.	I stand up for what I believe to be the truth and the honest way of doing things.
	I believe in always striving to do the right thing.	I will always do what is right over what is easy.	
Respect	I believe in honouring other people's opinions.	I will actively listen to what others have to say.	I practise empathic listening, to fully hear what others are telling me.

(Continued)

Table 1.1 Values and Intent (*Continued*)

Value	Belief	What intentions	What behaviour
Diversity	I believe diversity enriches the community.	I will educate myself on different cultures.	I listen to others from different cultures. I read books and listen to music from and about different cultures.
Connection	I believe in striving to connect well with others.	I prioritise making time for others. I prioritise understanding others.	I set time aside to concentrate on having quality relationships. I actively listen to what others are saying.
Compassion	I believe that everyone is trying their best with the information they have available at the time.	I will meet others from a loving and caring place in my heart.	I demonstrate caring and compassionate behaviours towards others.

This is an exercise you can come back to, and we encourage that you revisit this time and time again, as it takes a great deal of self-reflection and processing in order to really pin down what is most important to us as individuals. As authors, we are at the advantage of having had many hours of psychological therapy and self-reflection in which to consider our own sets of values and still this is an ongoing journey; as with every new life experience and relational interaction, our values and/or our interpretation of those values can change and take on different meanings over time. The important thing is for you to identify and honour your own core values in order to celebrate what makes you *you*. When we are living in a way which aligns with our values we shall optimise our wellbeing. So, those values we carry with us, at work, at play, and in all relational connections with others are significant on many levels.

Making time to explore our personal values is important in the context of building and maintaining good relationships with families, as by doing so we are able to be more in line with our authentic self. Being authentic and genuine in our thoughts and behaviours allows those around us to trust in what we say and do. Trust is an essential component to any relationship, and being true and living within our values is a core feature of what facilitates trust.

Values, beliefs and behaviours

By having an initial look at some of our own key values, we have identified some general themes which impact on our own thoughts, feelings and behaviours. This is relatively straight-forward as we self-reflect. Where this becomes far more complex is when we consider the millions of variables and possibilities that exist when individuals interpret their values through their beliefs and consequent behaviours, and what happens in relationships when we all have our own different beliefs, understandings and possibly even conflicting values systems. Some of you have 30 students in your class, each with their own unique and evolving set of values, beliefs and behaviours, then there's your colleagues; and we haven't even started talking about parents yet. We hope you can see why it is so important that you, the individual, and your values, do not get swamped and lost in this vast jungle of ideologies we call 'school'. Alas, let's go on to consider how our values play out in our day-to-day lives.

Exercise 1.2

Knowing me, knowing you

We invite you to examine a typical Friday, or pick a day that you work at school. Think about your own values and belief systems as they play out from the moment you wake up. In doing so you might consider your 'oughts and nots'. These are your own personal set of rules for things that you believe you ought to do, or should not do.

1   Use the template in Table 1.2 and write your own list. We have given you a sample of Year 6 teacher Mrs Brown's answers, to get you started.

Table 1.2   Sample of personalised oughts and nots

Behaviour	Reason	Belief	Value
My alarm goes off at 5am and I go for a run.	If I don't get up early I miss my chance to get my run in before work.	It is healthy for my body and mind to exercise and have fresh air to start the day.	Self care and nurturing is vital and important to me.
Before I run I open all the curtains in the house.	I was brought up that you do not leave the curtains closed in daylight.	My neighbours might think there was something wrong or I was lazy if I left the curtains closed, and I believe it'd be lazy of me.	Despite it annoying my wife, as she does not wake until 6am, I care about how other people view me and don't want to be seen as lazy. I am proud.
I eat breakfast together with my wife in the kitchen, and we flick through social media and have the news on TV.	It's important for us to share meals together, when we can, and we enjoy that time in the morning, commenting on the latest news.	This is quality and enjoyable time, that sets us up for the day – with good food, current affairs, and conversation on our thoughts and feelings.	Sharing meals and media is a fun way to connect with my wife and it's important to enjoy time together in marriage.

(Continued)

Table 1.2 Sample of personalised oughts and nots (*Continued*)

Behaviour	Reason	Belief	Value
I car share with three other teachers to get to school.	We are doing our bit for the environment.	There are too many cars on the road and car share is also economical.	Looking after the environment and the world we live in, is a high priority in my life.
On arriving at school, I go straight to my classroom and start preparing.	I could have coffee in the staffroom, but avoid going there in case I get caught up in conversation.	My time is precious and I want that preparation time uninterrupted before registration. My teaching time is of best quality if I prepare well.	For me, I prioritise being well prepared for my students, over socialising with my team. I work hard to do the best job I can for my students. I always give my best. And so on…

It can be a lot of fun and very interesting examining our answers, as they can also help us recognise where our behaviours come from, and if the things that we do, think or believe actually fit with our present core values, or whether they are old patterns that no longer serve us. We can break down our daily patterns, behaviours and beliefs to become more aware of our own individual value systems – and where our behaviours are consistent or differ to those values. When our values are compromised, it can have a detrimental effect on our wellbeing as well as our sense of agency (more of which in Chapter 7). In most of our professional lives, there shall be times that we experience this, so it is important we have strategies to protect us from this. Our values are what calls us to action, what motivates us and what makes us great at what we do. We get a sense of purpose and accomplish satisfaction, contentment and pleasure when we feel we are acting in line with our core values and this has a ripple effect from the inside out.

Now, let's take the examples above and consider the many different combinations of behaviours, reasons, beliefs and values that might be possible for people that Mrs Brown comes into contact with on a Friday morning.

Mrs Brown's Friday morning connections

On her morning run, Mrs Brown always says hello and sometimes chats to a woman of her own age, who she assumes to share the same healthy living values, as she too runs in the fresh morning air, at the same park, every day. However, the fellow runner, in actual fact, has an extreme fear of gaining weight. She hates running and she knows it is making her mental and physical health suffer, as she has not consumed enough calories to fuel her body. Her outward behaviour appears to be motivated by the same values, beliefs and reasons as Mrs Brown's (from Mrs Brown's perspective), and so making this assumption, the two runners have never made a real connection – as their thinking and motivation are coming from such different directions.

At breakfast time, Mrs Brown is feeling good and refreshed after her run and a shower. Mrs Brown's wife, however, is thoroughly hacked-off because once again, she's been woken too early. She's not in the mood to engage fully in conversation with Mrs Brown, and so she welcomes the distraction of social media and the news being on TV, so she can ready herself for her day at her own pace and talk about things she is interested in, rather than running or school. Mrs Brown's wife does share the same values to some extent as Mrs Brown, however, her beliefs, reason and motivation are certainly different.

Mrs Brown is part of a car-share with Miss Lopez, Mr Lemon and Ms Hobbs. Mrs Brown and Miss Lopez take turns to drive the group of four teachers. Miss Lopez likes being part of a car-share for the social time and connection with the others for their journey and appreciates the environmental and cost saving factors. Miss Lopez likes all her colleagues, but her religious and cultural views include the openly negative judgement of same sex marriage, consumption of alcohol and gambling, among many other things. Mr Lemon is on a driving ban for a court conviction of drunk driving. He has no other way of getting to work and doesn't care about the environment nor the car conversations from his colleagues, which he endures, finding them to be dull. Ms Hobbs doesn't have her own car. She isn't great with money and gambles her wages away, so she can't afford a car nor public transport to get to work. Miss Lopez feels continually disappointed that the four colleagues don't socialise outside of these car journeys, she can't understand why they have never truly connected and haven't become friends.

Finally, when Mrs Brown eventually gets into school, and heads straight to her classroom, she gets incredibly frustrated with the SENCO, who believes he is being helpful by popping in to see how she is doing and having a little check-in chat. Mrs Brown attempts to be polite, but really just wants rid of him so she can get on with her work. The SENCO shares one of Mrs Brown's values about the importance of mental and physical health and wellbeing. Only Mrs Brown runs in order to achieve this, whereas the SENCO believes that peer support and reaching out to connect with your team, is essential for any teacher's wellbeing. The SENCO feels hurt and rejected that Mrs Brown's body language shows that she is not receptive to his gestures, nor his attempt to engage with her.

2   What are your thoughts and assumptions of our characters: Mrs Brown and her connections? What judgements have you made? Do you have a liking or dislike for any of them? There's no right or wrong, just insight. Hold onto those insights as you go through the book.

3   Now, please take a moment to reflect on a situation where it has come to your attention that a colleague or friend has differing values to yours. What happens to the way you think? In particular, what assumptions and judgements do you make about the individual, and how do those assumptions affect the way in which you communicate? And, ultimately, what happens to your relationship with that person? Is it easy to trust somebody who does not share your values?

Rules

Our values and beliefs directly shape our own internalised set of rules. These rules develop as a set of principles and expectations, which govern the way we conduct ourselves as well as the assumptions we make of others. For example, somebody who holds 'honesty' as a core value might believe that it is wrong to tell a lie. The resulting rule might be 'People should always tell the truth'. Note that this is a rule extended beyond the personal, to the collective. Should this rule be broken, by the rule maker themselves, or by another, there is a judgement made based on the implication of that behaviour in reference to the values of the rule-breaker e.g. 'liars are bad people'. On the breaking of one's own rule, there may be an experience of guilt and shame. Many people shun those words, finding them negative and unhelpful emotions. However, for self-regulation and the abiding by healthy rules, guilt and shame can serve us well, and help us access our conscience. Therefore, all emotions are helpful in drawing our attention to something; it's the responses to those emotions that are either helpful or unhelpful. Furthermore, the more we gain personal understanding of these responses, the more we are empowered within each given situation.

Let's think about rules, from the inside out, and how this all relates to our relationships with our pupils and their families.

- We each have our own values system as part of our core being and identity.
- People hold unique sets of beliefs based on their values.
- Thoughts and behaviours are consequences of our beliefs.
- We develop rules which we attempt to live by, in keeping with our way of thinking, behaviour, beliefs and values.
- We desire that other people live by our rules too, thus sharing in our thinking, behaviours, beliefs and values.

It's easy to see the problems here, and the good news is: the solution is not so hard to come by, so long as we keep awareness that ours is one bespoke set of rules, relating to our own values systems; and it is extremely important that each and every one of us feels that we have the right to live and express ourselves in a way which is congruent to our core values and true self (within the law). How we go about doing this, without enticing complete anarchy and chaos, starts with you. Here is a step-by-step guide as to how this unfolds:

Step 1

You are now actively engaged in self-reflection and considering your own value systems, associated beliefs, thoughts, behaviours and internal rules. With this self-awareness, you can consider your personal needs within your job role. What are the things that are important to you as a teacher, and how might you have your needs met within your job role?

Step 2

With self-awareness you can ensure that your classroom is a safe place for freedom of speech, working within the school values. For example, you might explain to your class, from the first point of meeting, that there is a difference between saying whatever we like, and having freedom to think and express our ideas and questions in a respectful way. You can encourage openness and curiosity that is from a kind and accepting place, and with an open heart and mind, demonstrate to your class that adults learn every day, and that the class teach you as much as you teach them, in sharing their unique experiences. Together, you are on a journey of new discoveries and understanding many different world perspectives.

Step 3

Invite your class to share with you the things that are important to them, and encourage them to consider their personal and individual values. We shall provide some specific guidance according to Key Stages at the end of this chapter.

Step 4

Working in groups then as a whole class, acknowledge the different types of values that exist and look at grouping values into categories (specific guidance according to Key Stages to follow). Calculate where differences in values exist as well as looking at common values, which you can then use to inform your class, and wider school rules.

Step 5

Emphasise the importance of health, safety and mental wellbeing, and discuss the reasons that laws exist to ensure people are treated in a fair manner. Discuss as a class the rules within the law and which values these rules may have developed from. Consider the changes within law over time and how this reflects societal values.

Step 6

Ensure that your class have their individual opinions heard, and then their collective voice heard and represented amongst the wider school. School assemblies are a great opportunity for this.

Step 7

Seek parental input. This may seem quite far down the line. However, until we give our students the opportunity to think about their value systems, we cannot expect them to have meaningful conversations about values with us or their families. Again, we have specific Key Stage appropriate guidance for exactly how this can be achieved, but this is an important opportunity to provide, regardless of how you do it. This brings us to considering the different types of values that we might hold.

Types of values

Of course, we can categorise values into types, and here are a few, but this is also a worthwhile exercise for self and wider learning.

- Ethical
- Spiritual
- Cultural
- Social
- Familial
- Relational
- Political

For each *type* of value we can consider things from an individualistic stance, through to a global point of view. Always, however, we must champion equality, diversity and fair representation of values.

The term *Fundamental British Values* entered government policy and the world of education in 2011, being defined as:

1) Democracy, the rule of law, individual liberty and mutual respect and tolerance for those with different faiths and beliefs.

2) Mutual respect and tolerance includes encouraging students to respect other people with particular regard to the protected characteristics of the Equality Act [2010].

(Department for Education published 27th November 2014 www.gov.uk)

It is against the law to discriminate against someone because of: age, disability, gender reassignment, marriage and civil partnership, pregnancy and maternity, race, religion or belief, sex, sexual orientation ... but furthermore, we have a huge responsibility in teaching this good stuff. So, it becomes all the more important that we are able to see our own blind spots and assumptions that we make around the values, beliefs, reasons and behaviours of those who we come into contact with, directly or indirectly, in order that we are fair and protect others from discriminatory and damaging ways of being.

It is not good enough that policy and legislation guidelines are pinned to a wall somewhere in your school. At the core of British values is that each and every one of us has a responsibility to do the very best we can, in teaching, displaying and upholding the richness of diversity in our social, cultural and religious values. So, at every level, from classroom lessons, to staffing and policy meetings, to management and school governance and beyond to the wider communities in which you teach, we must be thinking *values*.

The Black Lives Matter campaign continues to highlight the damage to society when we lack the self-awareness that allows us to have a wider perspective, wisdom or insight. Without this insight, we fail to act according to our values when we see things going wrong or perhaps may fail to notice when something could be done better. When we are aware and notice these things, we also must *act*, and encourage our students and their families to do so too. We shall provide direct guidance around this in the next chapter. There are many incredibly powerful things that can happen within your classroom when we celebrate diversity, and hold high the Fundamental British Values as individuals, with a whole-school approach, and taking that to the wider school community through the families belonging to our schools. Working from the inside out is the most effective way of doing this.

Managing conflicting values or beliefs

Prevention is always more preferable than cure, and even with our best efforts to hear one another, we must pay attention to the smallest of voices as well as those loud and proud, and use our self-awareness to ensure we are not mishearing or tone-deaf to narratives we are ignorant of. There is always going to be disagreement around belief systems and ideologies as long as there are human beings. It's inevitable, and not surprising, but despite this, teachers spend a huge amount of time working with families to resolve disharmony, when it is perceived that school, or perhaps more directly, you (the teacher) has acted, behaved or taught in a way that is not fitting with the values belonging to a particular family. This is a matter that causes great upset in school communities, and has potential to spread toxicity to wider society if solutions are not sought. Amongst the more emotive issues that raise parent complaints are when the customs according to a certain value or belief are not adhered to by school, for example, dietary requirements belonging to certain groups, such as vegan, halal, or kosher options not being provided as an alternative in a cookery class. Another common issue is the perception that one's child is being excluded from class group activity based on a special educational need. Generally speaking, parents tend to approach their child's teacher when they feel their child/family is not being treated fairly.

Exercise 1.3

Family values

1 Please take a moment now to reflect on a time you know of, when a parent raised an issue about something happening in school that they were not happy about.
2 Now consider the dialogue between parent and teacher on this matter. In doing this you might find you have a kind of script of what is being said. Rather than focus on what is being said, see if you can unpick the belief behind what is said, and what the underlying value is. What is the belief or values-rule that the parent feels has been violated? How does the teacher (possibly you) view this differently?
3 Now find where the common ground and shared values are for the parent and the teacher. Are there any beliefs and values that are fundamentally different, and if so, do the school values help connect the parent and teacher?

It is far easier to do this in hindsight, and from a logical and analytical perspective, with the heat of emotion removed from the dialogue. But what does that tell you about the way in which we are often thrown into these unplanned situations, when a parent unexpectedly confronts a teacher? It can feel rather like an attack or being ambushed... we must defend ourselves and our school. Our natural defences kick in and we are instantly on high alert, feeling that we and our values are under threat. We feel our integrity as a professional, holding the highest standards of professionalism, as well as a person, with strong values on fairness, is coming into question. It's a tough place to start any neutral type of dialogue or to problem solve effectively for the family you are now faced with. To most of us, this scenario is all too familiar. If you are a student teacher, perhaps less so, but that's OK, because we can all get better prepared right now.

Managing unexpected confrontations

Firstly, in the immediacy of an unexpected confrontation, make it very clear, in a calm voice, that you really would like to hear more and fully what the parent needs to tell you, and suggest when and where it is possible to have this conversation (it may not be immediately possible if the parent comes to you first thing in the morning before the school day begins, so offer the first available opportunity you have, clarifying that it is very important to you to listen to what the parent has to say). Do *not* be defensive or enter into any kind of debate.

Once in an appropriate setting for the conversation, listen without interruption to the parent. Perhaps repeat back what the parent is saying to ensure your understanding, at which point you can ask if you can take some notes to help you resolve the issue. Ask the parent questions about what they would desire as an outcome, and open questions about how they, their child/wider family are feeling about the situation they describe. Don't disagree or argue with the parent. We repeat, do not become defensive. Listen, show empathy and compassion for how they feel. Use supportive phrases such as 'I'm so sorry you feel like that' and 'please, take your time, I'm here to listen and hope I can help'.

Reassure the parent that you are taking what they say seriously, and offer them a reasonable time frame in which you shall respond to the conversation you have had/ information they have shared with you – outlining any obvious actions that you need to take. At this point, ask the parent to please continue to let you know about any concern that they have. Be absolutely clear that you value their input and openness as an important member of the school community, and that you appreciate them talking to you. This may not be how you are actually feeling. In fact, depending on the context or content of the grievance, you may be feeling all kinds of emotions, and you may completely disagree with what the parent has said to you. However, on the initial connection, the most important thing in terms of developing your working relationship is really hearing the experience of the person who is talking to you, whilst safe in the knowledge that you are protecting yourself and your own values.

Then, the absolute most important thing that you do next is that you act. We can practise all the best listening skills, with self-awareness, a calmness in tone, using empathy, and understanding, but if we fail to actually follow through in taking action, and feeding back to the parent, we have immediately broken trust, and severed that connection... and then we really do have a problem. We can hear you sigh 'but what if the expectation of the parent is completely unrealistic?'. This is where our values system comes directly to play. We have time to reflect on what the parent is telling us, and what they are feeling. We can then analyse using Exercise 1.3 and identify our shared values. On feeding back to the parent about what you are doing to take action, is taking the raised concern, and lifting it out of that conflict zone that was initially between you. You lift up that issue, and you place it out before you and the parent, who metaphorically are now side by side, addressing that issue together. *Together*, parent and teacher, connected by your shared values, you can figure out a common goal, and tackle the issue – rather than one another. Your values are at the core of this beautifully functional relationship.

Developing a value based community

To simply state what values you hold as a teacher or as a school, implies an assumption that everyone shares the same definition, understanding and interpretation of what those values actually mean. Input and opinion must be sought from every member of the school community, and that means parents too. It is vitally important that all school policies and procedures align with the values shared by the school community, and where this is not possible it needs to be clear as to why a policy contradicts the values. *Incongruence* is a big connection breaker.

When it comes to developing values for your school or classroom, it's a good idea to start with student consultation. Students are much more likely to buy into a set of values when they have had a role in developing them from the start. Simultaneously, opinions can be sought from families, through various channels of communication including online surveys with questions devised from the data collected from student opinions.

Following appropriate consultation, displaying a clear message that links the school values to a set of beliefs and expectations of behaviours from staff and students based on those values, gives an open framework of how an organisation works, as well as helping everyone to understand what the consequences are when those expectations aren't adhered to.

'We selected a school for our son based on the values that the school promoted on their website and on our initial visit to the school. The values were made very clear and everybody seems to buy into that, which makes it a lovely community that we felt instant belonging to.' Aarav and Aadya, parents of Dev, Year 2

The above exemplifies the ultimate goal of any school community, this is the kind of feedback that says 'we've got it right'. The school has made it clear what their values are and what that means. They have also cultivated a community where everyone buys into the set of values, lives by them and the community generates a sense of belonging. Knowing that we share values and those around us are invested in living by those common aims, makes us feel safe, and secure. Doesn't every family want that? As teachers, parents are trusting us with what's most precious to them, and the environment we create must elevate confidence at all three sides of the student-teacher-parent triad, that school is a safe place to be.

If a school community displays a set of values, there needs to be a clear narrative of what that means for them. By using the previous table, this gives you a framework of how to build a clear message and demonstrate to everyone what you believe and how you demonstrate that as a community. For example:

- **Value:** Team spirit.
- **Belief:** As a school we believe in camaraderie amongst school, families and wider community.
- **What intentions:** To work closely with parents and families through constantly striving towards a continued open and inclusive environment where everyone is welcome.
- **What behaviour:** Clear line of communication between teacher and parent through the use of school homework books. Parents evening. Regular newsletters.

This example clearly shows how a value has led to a belief which the school feels represents team spirit, how they are working with this belief, and what that specifically means (the specific things done as a school/class/teacher is part of this value). Using this method not only communicates clearly the value and beliefs but, most importantly, what people want to know what that means for them; this also manages expectations. This workable framework offers an effective way of asking for feedback and promoting regular involvement of families with questions such as:

- 'Do you feel our school has a team spirit?'
- 'Do you feel a sense of camaraderie?'
- 'If not, what could be done to enable you to feel a greater sense of team spirit?'

The framework doesn't only offer a way of communicating your values effectively, it gives you a simple and effective means of reaching out to the wider school community, and gaining parental feedback to help inform the school values and subsequent rules.

When it comes to building your own school community values you can use the framework provided to work through step by step, involving all families, staff and pupils. Send out a questionnaire and ask what people value, what beliefs they hold and what are the expected actions within the values. From a blank table you can start to insert the feedback into the relevant sections. Not everyone will provide the data exactly as you want them to with an explicit set of values, it may be more of a belief, a behaviour or an expectation that you get given. However, that's ok because it's still data you can collect and work out how you can demonstrate opinions and identify the needs of your families, as you go through this process. It is all helpful insight and information.

Conclusion

Demonstrating a clear set of values, which are consistently adhered to, is a foundational element of trust and security. Trust and security are key factors in the development and maintenance of effective relationships. Understanding our values and the way in which they affect our thoughts, behaviours and feelings is central to nurturing the authentic self, forming meaningful relationships and well-bonded communities. The framework within this chapter gives you an opportunity to further your insight into what values are important to you, your associated beliefs, intentions and behaviours, and how this impacts on connections with others. Self-reflection and finding deeper personal understanding, alongside utilising the value, belief, intention, and behaviour framework, allows us to communicate a clear and congruent message, which will forge a far stronger starting point for relational connection. Identifying and addressing diversity in value systems is vital when it comes to connection. Having a clear set of values as a whole school community also sets the groundwork for parents making informed choices when selecting a school for their child which aligns with their family values. Having a clear set of values also keeps us focused on what really matters, which is invaluable when we are responding to change and/or difficult situations.

Resources

Student resources

KS1

Hands Are Not for Hitting by Martine Agassi
The Day the Crayons Quit by Drew Daywalt
The Hedgehogs – Because I Wanted to Play With You by Tamiko Pettee
The Thirsty Dragon by KL Piazza

KS2

Charlotte's Web by EB White
Kindness: A Treasury of Buddhist Wisdom for Children and Parents by Sarah Conover and Valerie Wahl
Big Thoughts for Little Thinkers by Daniel Thompson
Harry Potter series by JK Rowling

KS3/4

Freak the Mighty by Rodman Philbrick
Rules by Cynthia Lord
This Side of Home by Renee Watson
To Kill a Mockingbird by Harper Lee
The 7 Habits of Highly Effective Teens by Sean Covey

Teacher resources

Values Education in Schools: *A Resource Book for Student Inquiry* by Gilbert Burgh, Lyne Tilt McSporran and Mark Freakley
Dare to Lead by Brene Brown

Living Values Education Activities for Children Ages 3–7, Book 1; *Children Ages 8–14 Book 1*, and *Young Adults Book 1* (three separate books by Diana Hsu and Diane G. Tillman)

A Quiet Revolution: Encouraging Positive Values in Our Children by Frances Farrer Https://7mindsets.com

Parent resources

Set up a parent resource area within your school. Make this a calm and comfortable space where parents can easily access and get up to date information plus feel involved with the school. Have your school values and rules clearly displayed and feedback forms available for queries and input. Perhaps have a display board with pictures of the staff, including a bio, and some fun facts relating to each individual's core values and how these values play out.

Have a parent lending library including such books as:

7 Habits of Highly Effective Families by Stephen R. Covey

Why Love Matters by Sue Gerhardt

The Stepfamily Handbook by Karen S. Bonnell and Patricia L. Papernow

If I Could Tell You Just One Thing by Richard Reed

Books by Oliver James: *They F*** You Up, How Not to F*** Them Up* and *Love Bombing*

References

DfE (2014) *Promoting fundamental British values as part of SMSC in schools.* Available at: https://assets.publishing.service.gov.uk/government/uploads/system/uploads/attachment_data/file/380595/SMSC_Guidance_Maintained_Schools.pdf (accessed 9 August 2021).

2

COMMUNICATION

-- Chapter objectives --

- What is the importance of first impressions?
- To reflect on opportunities for communicating with families
- To understand non-verbal communication
- To explore authentic communication and advance listening skills
- To explain Carl Rogers' core conditions for personal growth
- To reflect on dealing with conflict
- To consider how to deliver a successful parents' evening.

Introduction

We hope that you appreciate why 'values' precedes 'communication', and that you will keep exploring 'values' as we work through our values based connection model. Communication is our next key feature to work with. In order to define this within the context of your education setting, let us first consider all the ways that our school communicates with parents and families. If we take, for example, a new family looking to join your school mid-term, their first point of contact is likely to be communication with administrative staff to arrange a visit to the school. First impressions can really last, and from the first point of communication, families want to feel that your school is the right place for their child, and a place that they can trust to deliver education in line with their values. Referring back to Chapter 1, we can see the various ways that our school can visibly display and communicate our values, which is a great starting point. However, it is the interpersonal connection made on that first opportunity to welcome a family that is most crucial in how a family will feel about your school. So how can we make these first meetings with your school really count?

First impressions count

You'll be aware of your own school's systems for new intakes, and for showing families around whilst giving information and answering questions specific to your unique education setting. It is usually best that it is a head teacher, assistant head or head of year, that takes this role. Schools that task their managers to greet new families are immediately giving the message that the family is important and worth the time of their senior staff. A smart school shall also select an individual who has excellent interpersonal skills, and the ability to quickly form effective relationships with parents, because that is going to be the deal clincher under those first impressions.

> 'I was apprehensive about my children starting at such a huge school, so anticipated that our welcome tour might be pretty daunting and a bit scary for my family. However, the assistant head was absolutely lovely, and everybody already knew my children by name. We were made to feel special and that we belonged at that school, within minutes of being there, and the warm, genuine and personal touch as well as the close interest the staff took in our family, gave us the best start we could have hoped for.'
> Mary-Anne, parent of children in Years 10, 8 and 7.

Focusing on making an authentically heart-felt connection with your families is undoubtedly going to enhance relationships. However, perhaps as a teacher, you have little involvement with families at this initial stage, so it may be more helpful to think of the opportunities that you *do* have, to directly communicate with families.

The bearer of bad news

When you stop and think about the opportunities you do have to communicate with parents, there may be very few. For many teachers, the only time you may engage with parents is a 10-minute slot on parent-teachers evening. Other than this opportunity (whereby you may not indeed meet all significant parents or family members of your students), sadly the only other time (at present) that you are communicating directly with parents is when something has gone wrong, and you need to give the bad news, and perhaps request intervention from home. The impact of this, is that when a parent receives direct communication from a teacher, for example being requested to 'step aside for a chat' on school collection, or receiving a telephone call from school, the parent's immediate internal response is 'Oh no, what has happened? What has my child done wrong?. Parents often experience feelings of anxiety or dread in that moment when their child's teacher instigates contact. This environment of stress and worry is far from the optimal conditions required for helpful communications, and we are sure that many of you know exactly the feeling of being in this situation, of bringing the bad news ... it's not comfortable, right? To help with natural but uncomfortable situations, we can ensure the communications we have with the parents of our students is compassionate, before building on that. Here is our practical guide to making this happen in your classroom, for your school.

Creating communication opportunities

Let us now look at some examples on how to create communication opportunities.

- Introduce yourself, and communicate to the families of your students, from as early as possible, the means in which they can get in touch with you, with any queries or anything they wish to discuss – offering email addresses, or ways to sign up for a chat, request a phone call, whatever way you can work it within your school. A letter and email with this information, and who else they might be able to communicate with at school, is extremely helpful, especially if your child has eight teachers and a parent may not know where to start.
- Check that there is one clear point for parents to pick up any important messages, so they don't become overwhelmed by too much or fractured communications from multiple sources. Many schools keep everything on the main website, and send emails/texts with vital reminder info.
- Take any opportunity possible to communicate positive things to parents about their child's learning, development and generally observations of great attitudes and qualities you see in your students. Some schools have reward systems in place, and parents receive celebratory letters or emails congratulating their family for successes.
- Make your communications positive, personalised, brief and regular. Frequent, genuine, short and sweet messages are more effective than one long generic letter to begin each term.
- Plan and host presentation afternoons or evenings for your class to showcase work that they have been doing, and invite families into the classroom to be entertained by the students, giving you and your team a chance to chat with parents as well as an opportunity to really build on student-family-school relations, by coming together as a community, at an enjoyable event.
- Ensure that working parents have equal opportunities to engage with school. This might mean arranging a telephone meeting with those that will normally not be available within the school day to communicate. You may need to have a chat about how you might work around that, with other carers or mutually convenient means of communication.
- Link with your SENCO to ensure that parents and families with special needs are reached out to and appropriate measures taken to ensure a strong line of communication is established for families that might have extra communication challenges. Checking if information can be made available in any languages spoken by parents belonging to your school, can also help accessibility.

These are all examples of things that you can make happen, for your students and their families, and by doing so create a culture whereby everybody feels more able to communicate in a supportive way. We aim to create a shift from the unpleasant associations of 'parent being summoned to the headteacher's office', to a new and positive experience and associated feelings on communications with school. Please do remember too, to have fun where you can, in any of the communications you make. It is wise to be mindful that when parents communicate with schools, or even think about schools, they bring with them their associations of their own school life and experiences. As teachers we can't possibly know the educational history of all of our families, however, it helps to be mindful that many parents find the school environment and all that comes with it, stressful. If you can help create a fun and relaxed communication space, you'll enable rich and rewarding connections with your families. So, now that we have considered improving the opportunities for communication, let's take a closer look at our communication skills.

Goals in communication

The ultimate communication goal is when the message in one person's head is sent and received exactly as it was intended to be understood, by sender and recipient. When we are being communicated to, ideally we are able to gather information effectively in order that we get a clear idea of what message the sender is trying to convey. This is where understanding your values and beliefs, from the start, can be very insightful in addressing how those values and the communication of those, can help or hinder relationships. It's always helpful to keep this in mind when sending or receiving any information – ask yourself, 'Am I explaining myself in a way that is going to be received the way it's intended? Do I need more information to get a clear picture of what I am receiving?'.

There are many different forms of communication used within modern education, and as our technology advances there are likely to be many more. However, we're going to focus here on face to face communication, as within the context of schools, it is where most difficulties can arise, due to emotional responses. The ideas and strategies we explore here can be transferred to other forms of communication.

--- Exercise 2.1 ---

Body language

In this exercise we invite you to expand your self-awareness. There are three key components in face-to-face communication: the language we use, tone of voice, and body language. It's widely believed that the brain puts much more weight on body language than the other two aspects, when interpreting what is being communicated. Albert Mehrabian and Susan R. Ferris' research (1967) identified that only 7% of communication is the words spoken when interpreting the meaning. This is why understanding yourself is so important as a starting point, as when communicating with others, it's your body that will give away responses that you may not want to communicate. As body language is so important we're going to start with that, working from the inside out. Let's reflect on each of the following, noting down our observations, which we'll come back to reflect upon through the chapter.

What happens to your body when:

1   you are feeling defensive
2   you are talking to someone you don't like
3   you are talking to someone you like
4   you feel confident
5   someone is saying something you don't like.

Once we understand our physical reactions, we can manage them effectively in order to optimise communication. The importance of this can't be stressed enough, as if your body language is incongruent with what you are saying, your words are meaningless and trust is compromised, resulting in damaged relationships. It is not enough to profess what values we hold dear and what we believe, we have to communicate that we are true to those values. As the old saying goes 'actions speak louder than words', and it is not just our overt behaviours that might communicate for us, but the subtle facial expressions, postures, mannerisms and gestures that create their own signals and visual cues in the observer.

Exercise 2.2

Mind your tone and language

Voice tone and language also play a role within the complexity of neurolinguistic perception. Let's consider this, reflecting again on the questions from Exercise 2.1, thinking about tone and language. Again, we'll revisit this as we work through the chapter and further on in the book. Please note your responses now, with attention to clarity of speech, voice modulation, pitch, volume and the type of language used – is it casual, formal, questioning, or informative, metaphorical or direct?

The reason we ask you to join us in your reflection is that body language, tone and the words we choose, not only impact when we are the sender of communication, but also in our responses to receiving communication from others. In other words, these skills will also affect how effectively you listen. We can learn from this, that regardless of the factual content intended in the message being sent and received, there is such variation in the possible delivery and interpretations of the original core message. To be the best communicators we can be, we must always be striving for authenticity.

Let us again take a moment to self-reflect and make some notes on Exercise 2.3.

Exercise 2.3

The search for authenticity

- When do you feel most at peace with the person you are (most authentic)?
- When do you feel less like yourself?
- Are there times when you feel unable to be authentic?
- Who do you know who, in your opinion, is most authentic? Take a moment to write down what makes that person authentic, reflecting on what you've learned in the previous chapter, and think about how they communicate. Be specific about body language, words, tone and actions.

Again, there are no right or wrong answers. These exercises are designed to guide your reflections and help you develop your authentic self, in order to communicate more effectively. This reflective process is important, as only with self-awareness can we truly be seen and heard, as well as being truly open to seeing and hearing others. This inner awakening of the senses deeply enriches our perceptions and ability to make meaningful connections, when our opportunities to communicate are limited. So we ask you to please be patient and work with the process as we build on your innate resources. The idea is that by putting in the groundwork now, your rewards will come, in the time you save down the line on miscommunications and misunderstandings, in and outside the classroom.

Listening

Before we can move on to look at managing the way we communicate, we need to understand how we listen. Do you consider yourself a good listener and if so what qualities do you feel make you a good listener? If you're not sure whether you are a good listener or not, think about someone you know who is and reflect on what qualities *make* them a good listener.

When it comes to listening, the goal is to understand the message. This sounds simple enough. However, advanced communication is built on effective listening, because if we can't fully understand what someone is saying to us, we're not able to respond effectively. The process of listening is complex. Our brains upload what is being communicated, hear what is being said, read what is left unspoken simultaneously with our personal filters of judgements and assumptions all interacting to form an interpretation.

Here are the steps to good listening:

1   Listen with the intention of understanding from the perspective of the messenger.
2   Hold self-awareness of personal responses and judgements that may alter the understanding of the intent of the messenger.
3   Start with the intention that it's your responsibility to gain understanding.

If we listen with the intention of understanding from the perspective of the other person, we're more likely to be open and receptive to what they are telling us, directly or indirectly. This skill, empathic listening, is not widely practised within society. Most people are listening from their own perspective, which is how our brains are designed to work. The complex brain draws on past information to relate and understand the new information. However, our understanding then becomes clouded by assumptions and/or emotions based on prior experiences, leading to the potential of not fully hearing what's being communicated to us, in the present.

Exercise 2.4

The empathic listener

Empathic listening is also a key ingredient in building trust. Trust is built on the small consistent actions within our relationships that altogether create a feeling of security in the beholder. When somebody gives us information and they *don't* feel heard, it can develop a sense of doubt about whether that information is safe with us. We invite you to note a time when you've spoken to somebody and you were left feeling unheard. Take note of what they communicated in their response. Was it mainly verbal or non-verbal communication? The non-empathic listener may:

- Fail to pay attention to the messenger / focus elsewhere.
- Make dismissive facial expressions, inappropriate to an understanding response.
- Reply from their own perspective which you struggle to relate to.
- Make assumptions they know what you are going through due to having a similar experience.
- Talk at you rather than really address what you've said.

Do any of these examples resonate with you? Again, think about a time when you may have done any of the above, professionally or personally. We are only human, and there will be times our minds are pulled elsewhere and we don't give the person the attention needed to fully understand their situation. That's ok, as long as we notice and have awareness of this, we can manage the situation. It's when this goes unnoticed there will be irreparable damage. We will not get everything perfect all of the time. However, the more we invest in interpersonal relations, using the strategies within this book, the better we will get and the quicker we will be able to respond effectively to others.

Non judgemental listening

Being non judgemental is an essential skill when it comes to listening effectively, however, it's also an impossible act. Our brains are hardwired to make judgements, and as educators it's an important part of what we do. So, being 'non judgemental' means: Not allowing our judgements to affect the way we communicate. It's listening in an open and receptive way, with the purpose of wanting to understand from the perspective of the other person, not with the intention of resolving the issue, that will come later. We have to enter communication with the full intention to understand. Resolution will come automatically but can only be effective if you fully understand the problem.

Carl Rogers and the core conditions for personal growth

In the 1940s, psychologist Carl Rogers developed his model of person-centred therapy, believing that for any person to mentally develop in growth and fulfilment, they must be met with core conditions including empathy, unconditional positive regard, and congruence. This means that the very best outcomes can be achieved when listeners, be they psychological therapists or educators, are compassionate, understanding and genuine. When these conditions are in place, it is possible for desired outcomes to come about organically. In teaching we often use the metaphor of sowing seeds, providing the optimal conditions for their growth through careful nurturing, through understanding the needs of the plant, and the climatic effects that may hinder or help growth. We hope for our seeds to flourish, and we deeply care about this. These values are held common by every good teacher and parent there ever was and ever shall be. So, when issues arise causing a parent and teacher to feel upset about any kind of school matter, it can often mean there has been misunderstanding and breakdown in communications. On addressing these issues, and creating an opportunity for effective communication, you can facilitate growth from the inside out, not just for the parent/s you are connecting with, but in your own understanding of that family, and their unique perspective. This is the best type of CPD you'll ever get.

Dealing with conflict

Despite paying attention and doing all we can do to promote effective communications, we will still face conflict from time to time, and this can be difficult. We all have varying levels of tolerance for dealing with conflict and how we manage confrontation. As professionals responsible for the education and wellbeing of children, accountability and scrutiny is very high. This too makes it more likely that there will be times when we have to manage conflict, with parents, or indeed other teachers and senior management. Anticipating those times puts us in a strong position to be prepared for this inevitability, and feel able to manage in those challenging times. This can help develop confidence, assertiveness and resilience both professionally and personally.

In Chapter 1 we looked at using our values base to address an issue side-by-side with the parent, rather than in conflict with one another. But if the situation can not be resolved in this manner, we need more strategies. We also need to consider what happens when the family have not approached school, or perhaps are completely unaware of an issue arising at school, that you are going to need to confront them with.

Create a new comfort zone

Most people do not enjoy conflict, and no teachers like being the bearer of bad news to parents. Finding these conversations difficult and uncomfortable is normal, but discomfort can result in avoidance. It's important we try as much as possible not to avoid conflict even if we find it excruciatingly awkward. You'll get a small sense of relief from avoiding it, but it will bring lasting challenges, and undermine your sense of agency in the long term (more about that in Chapter 7). So, let's extend our comfort zones into that where you can manage conflict with increased confidence.

1   First decide if the issue can be resolved at school, without the involvement of parents or families. Quite often, there are many steps that can be taken within school, and in making an action plan with the pupil/s concerned as to how to resolve the issue. You can then refer to the plan you have made when you contact parents, so you are presenting them with the solution (as agreed by you and the student) rather than the problem.

2   Try to avoid making a cold-call to a parent. If you are able to, email or message to request that the parent make an appointment to communicate with you as soon as is mutually convenient, and by the parent's preferred means (telephone or video call or face-to-face meeting). This gives the family autonomy (no feeling of being summoned to the office) and also reduces stress by demonstrating you have this situation under control – there is no urgency or need for anyone to panic.

3   Keep communicating with the student, using the core conditions, and encourage the student to take as much responsibility for the communication with their family as they feel comfortable with. Emphasise that you really want the best outcome for that student and their family, and that you want to make things better, not worse. By keeping an open and honest dialogue, whilst maintaining unconditional positive regard, empathy and congruence, you will undoubtedly build a relationship of trust with your student (even if they don't show this). Stick at it and be consistent. You are then leading by example, when you have the opportunity to talk to the parents about how you are managing things.

4   Ensure that you have all the facts about the incident/offence. Double-check that the student or their family have any additional information they want you to know with regard to this case.

5   If you have to communicate that there is a punishment involved for this student, think carefully about how you present this message. It is a very different thing to talk about school values, rules and consequences to breaches of contracts, than it is to state a crime and punishment. Avoid talking about 'good and bad' behaviours. There are choices, and there are opportunities to learn and reassess our choices. Try and focus on the qualities you can see in your student that will allow them to succeed in making effective choices.

6   Acknowledge the feelings of the parent, and their response to the situation you present. Reassure the parent that the school is there to support their family, and that you feel sure you can work through anything together, with the support of the wider school community. It's impossible for us to know what might be going on at home, and so vital that the parent feels school is friend and not foe.

Delivering a successful parents' evening

Parents' evening can be a challenge. You have ten minutes allocated and so much to say, in such a short time. This is an opportunity for you to manage relationships with parents and families, and the perfect time to make a good impression. It's likely that the pressure to get through what is required as well as sticking to the time allocated is going to put you in a stress response before the parents' evening has even started:

* Begin by putting yourself in an optimum state. Look at regulating your physical response to any stress you feel (more on this in Chapter 5).
* Manage expectations, acknowledge you only have a set amount of time and that you need to stick to that time as much as you can, but have your diary there and if anything can't be resolved in that time, plan a future meeting with those parents that need it.

- Depending on your existing relationship, you may choose to let the parents lead by asking if they have any specific areas they wanted to focus on, or questions they'd like to ask, at the start. It can feel overwhelming for parents that they get talked at for ten minutes and don't always feel heard because teachers have so many factors pulling for attention. Start by prioritising what you mutually need to discuss during the evening, manage expectations and have clear boundaries.
- You are experts at feeding back to parents about academic achievement, you've got that one covered.
- Most parents also want to know about character development and wellbeing. Again, this can feel overwhelming to go into depth about at parents' evening, but so important. We've added a take-away in the resource section of our website to cover this. It's a hand-out for parents covering aspects of their child's health and wellbeing, to enhance the amount of information you give without adding too much time to your already busy schedule.

Conclusion

We are communicating all the time, with every person we make any type of contact with, in our daily lives. We also give messages in what we do not communicate, and this can be problematic in connections with school families, and lead to misunderstanding. We can maximise the possibility for effective relationships by optimising opportunity for skilful communication, and being active in our listening, to enhance our understanding of what others are trying to communicate to us.

Resources

Student resources

KS1

The Ninja Life Hacks series by Mary Nhin
The My Dragon series by Steve Herman
Social Skills for Kids by Janine Halloran

KS2

Social Skills Activities for Kids by Natasha Daniels
Life Skills by Kelly Swift
Making Good Communications: A Sourcebook of Speaking and Listening Activities for 9–11 Year Olds by Catherine Dellamain

KS3/4

5 Steps to School Success by Julia C. Gilbert, audio book narrated by Eleanor Caudill. Playing this audio book to your class will help them communicate with parents, teachers and the wider school effectively. This could be made available in your parent resource library or on your school website.

Teacher resources

Addressing Adversity: Prioritising adversity and trauma-informed care for children and young people in England, YoungMinds: www.youngminds.org.uk/professional/resources/addressing-trauma-and-adversity/
Using Poetry to Promote Talking and Healing by Pooky Knightsmith
Teacher Communication: A Guide to Relational, Organisational and Classroom Communication by Ken W. White
How To Be Heard by Julian Treasure
4 Essential Keys to Effective Communication by Bento C. Leal
Online Assertiveness Course: www.cci.health.wa.gov.au/Resources/Looking-After-Yourself/Assertiveness

Parent resources

Again, in the parents' area and notice-boards both online and in your school buildings, make it very clear how parents can contact school and the ways in which they can communicate. You might want a communications board so that parents can clearly identify who to talk to about any particular matters, and how to get in touch with that person.
How to Talk So Kids Will Listen & Listen So Kids Will Talk by Adele Faber and Elaine Mazlish
Smart Parents: Parenting for Powerful Learning by Bonnie Lathram, Carri Schneider and Tom Vander Ark
The following website is also useful: www.gettingsmart.com and www.parentkind.org (accessed 13 October 2021).

References

Mehrabian, A. and Ferris, S.R. (1967) Inference of attitudes from non-verbal communication in two channels, *Journal of Consulting Psychology*, 31, 248–252.

3

COMPASSIoN

- To introduce compassion
- To understand and develop practical strategies to develop a compassionate mindset
- To examine how to enhance connections with parents and family through compassion
- To explore how compassion and empathy meet and differ
- To emphasise the importance of trust and respect
- To consider stress reduction and trouble through compassion.

Introduction

Chapter 3 continues to examine the interplay of adult behaviours that we find in school settings, now considering a deeper cognitive level of functioning: compassion. Within our model, compassion doesn't feature as a distinct section, rather it is the filter from one section to the other. In its own right, compassion is an inner experience that will deeply enhance the richness of relationships for any individual who learns how to exercise it. This is what brings depth to the connections we make with those around us, and allows us to understand and make sense of the experiences of others, even if those experiences are unfamiliar to us. As teachers, we want our students to have empathy and compassion for one another as well as for themselves. This goes beyond kindness that is more of an outward demonstration, such as good manners, for example, holding a door open for another. Compassion is a deeper and truer form which makes kindness second nature from the ability to empathise with another, and then to communicate and display this emotional connection in a caring way, with healthy self-awareness of personal boundaries. When we are compassionate towards one another, and with ourselves, amazing things happen. Again, considering our parent-teacher-child triad, we know that with compassion, our relationships are going to be stronger, and not only that, our understanding, communication and expression of our values will become more meaningful and heartfelt. However, is the way we practise compassion effective, in our professional or personal lives? And how do we teach and learn this stuff?

The empathic teacher

For the purposes of this book we are working with a particular definition of compassion (there are many types of compassion). Here though, compassion is the concern for the wellbeing of others, coupled with the desire to ease any suffering or distress. When compassion is done altruistically, it is done so purely from the perspective that it is the right thing to do, not for any other motive. We also want to explore self-compassion of the same type. However, to be able to ease suffering and distress, whether that be within others or oneself, we first have to be able to recognise it. It's also worth reflecting at this stage the difference between sympathy and empathy, which are both fundamental to compassion. Sympathy is to feel sorrow or sadness for the suffering of others, whereas empathy shares this aspect along with further insight into their personal situation. Now, as teachers you are already experts in doing this with your pupils. We shall start by looking at this in more detail and then see how to help you use all those skills you already have, introspectively and with others around you (namely, parents).

Let's take the example of Greta, a Year 2 student who approaches her teacher, Mr Popp, in tears as her favourite pencil has just broken. Had this happened to Mr Popp it wouldn't upset him and he would go and get another pencil from the stationary store. However, as a teacher he understands that to Greta, the broken pencil is a big deal. Mr Popp has immediate sympathy for Greta, he feels sad because she's so upset. At this stage, Mr Popp only has sympathy (sad she's upset) and compassion (as he desires to ease her suffering). He doesn't know the pencil was given to her by her auntie who she misses deeply because she has just moved overseas, so breaking this pencil is particularly upsetting for Greta. Mr Popp has compassion as he wants to make things better for Greta, so he is sensitive in figuring out what Greta needs to soothe the distress she is experiencing. Let's explore how having the interplay of sympathy, empathy and compassion all come together. Firstly, he addresses Greta's emotions and what she is feeling and feels sad that she's sad, which will all be displayed through his body language. Mr Popp has a deepened understanding of Greta, he knows about her auntie but doesn't know the connection to the pencil. The first step is recognising her pain and displaying sympathy. To have full empathy he needs to understand Greta's situation, so he asks her to tell him what's upsetting her so much about the pencil. Once she's told him who bought the pencil, this insight enables him to have empathy to then show compassion by working towards easing her suffering effectively. Mr Popp demonstrates his care and compassion, to not only Greta, and her classmates, and the TA in his class, but Greta is likely to be feeding back to her parents how much she likes Mr Popp, and how kind and caring he is.

It's important we understand the terms *empathy* and *sympathy* to describe the quality of Mr Popp's action. Of course, these definitions can take on different meanings in different contexts, but for the purpose of defining compassion, there is significance in the empathic connection. Metaphorically speaking, Greta has found herself in a hole, and she cries out to Mr Popp from this place deep in the ground. A *sympathetic* response from Mr Popp would be simply to recognise her suffering and to feel sad she's upset. Mr Popp's *empathic* response is to climb down into that hole, with his tool kit for getting out and meet Greta where she's at, to gather further information about the hole Greta is in. Then side by side, he can support her to find her way out, giving her trust and confidence that he understands and cares about what it's like for her down there. Mr Popp worked with Greta by sharpening the broken end and then she had two pencils to remind her of her auntie. Without the empathy he may have offered her another pencil, which wouldn't have eased her suffering, but by jumping in the hole to gather more knowledge he found an effective solution to ease her suffering.

With all of these concepts as human beings we see them through our own filters and perspective, but to be fully effective we have to recognise that the hole that you are in with the other person, belongs to the other person. In this example, the hole belongs to Greta, and Mr Popp is able to make that distinction and keep a professional boundary. As we follow someone on their emotional journey, our own brains seek to find meaning through our own personal experience. Within this process of association, a personal emotional response can be triggered, and if not managed can create emotional distress within oneself. Mr Popp does not become overwhelmed by the depth or the darkness of the hole he finds Greta to be in. This is important in order to help her. This is where the importance of self-awareness and working from the inside out is so important. In this example there is safety for Mr Popp in going down into the metaphorical hole, as he has a healthy self-awareness. The thought might cross his mind 'my own child has started nursery today, I hope she's not down a hole crying with nobody to help her'. Mr Popp is aware of his emotional response in the association he makes between Greta and his own daughter, and because he is aware of that involuntary emotional association, he is able to keep that in check and focus on Greta, *her* emotion and *her* narrative. Can you imagine how powerful this is for Greta, and for the class, to experience the autonomy this kind of pure empathic connection creates? Furthermore, not only does it enable Mr Popp to remain psychologically connected to Greta and optimise this interaction, it also keeps him psychologically well, safe from the dangers of over-identifying with someone else's pain.

Now reflect on your own interactions with your students, perhaps you have a Greta-situation in mind, or it might be a time when you have dealt with a student feeling broken-hearted at the end of a teen romance. Try and think of an example where you have been that empathic teacher, tending to a student's emotional need, in a truly altruistic way. As teachers, you have insight into the development of a child and adolescent; you will understand typical cognitive function at each stage of development. You may also know the individual student well, giving you further ability to empathise with any young person in your class, and a whole host of skills to ease the child's distress.

Learning to demonstrate care

As teachers, we care deeply about our students, and indeed their families. This goes beyond a professional duty of care, to sincere concern for those families. Find us a teacher who hasn't lost sleep out of this very real care. Yet all too often, we make the assumption that our students and families know how much we care and so we fail to effectively communicate this to them (as described in Chapters 1 and 2). Once we have this awareness there are simple things we can do to demonstrate compassion:

- Show an active interest in your pupil's out-of-school life. This might be hobbies, interests, family relations, holidays etc.
- Assume that your pupil has a complicated back story. From this perspective you can be sensitive to understanding the unique and diverse needs of the individual person.
- When needing to discuss an unkind behaviour, try and do so in a compassionate way. Chastising behaviour in front of a class can bring humiliation and shame. If you can gently approach the pupil in a one-to-one, they are going to learn more from your example of kindness in your approach.
- Forgive and forget. Once you have worked through any challenging matters you have had to deal with in terms of behaviour management, start afresh, giving the student or family involved a clear message of unconditional positive regard.
- Compliment and praise your students, colleagues and also students' parents, making positive statements about your observations and acknowledging their efforts.

And last, but definitely not least, demonstrate that you care for your class as them and as individuals, as well as their families at every opportunity. Ask how they are, and really listen, actively reflecting on assumptions you make about how they feel. Celebrate and commiserate together in their experiences. See the good in who they are, and let them see it too. Compassionate teaching comes from the heart, and will raise the self-esteem and self-worth of your students, as well as gaining their trust in you, as an adult who genuinely cares.

Trust and respect

Of course, we are not in the role of 'friend' to our students, and the boundary must always be clear. It can be helpful to define boundaries by engaging in dialogue about expectations.

Exercise 3.1

Expectations

As a teacher, make a list of your expectations from, a) your students, and b) parents/families. Consider aspects such as wellbeing, behaviour, attitude, attendance and so on. Then, write a list, c) of what you think your students' expectations are of you, and d) what you think your students' parents' expectations are of you.

You can use Exercise 3.1 for your personal or group reflection as professional development, and/or you could use this as an exercise with your class and include parents as part of a homework exercise. The data you collect will be unique to each group or individual. It provides a very helpful foundation for dialogue on which to build a framework of clarity so that everybody involved understands what they can reasonably expect from teachers, pupils, parents, and what might be expected of themself. What we have already learnt in Chapters 1 and 2 about communication and values, will of course be key elements underpinning the expectations discussed. In the words of Stephen Covey (1999), if we 'seek first to understand, and then to be understood' we are then working with sympathy and compassion. This ties in with the concepts explored in our earlier chapters, considering how we generate assumptions when we feel sympathy, and how it's easy to assume that we know what another person's sadness/suffering/sorrow is all about. By first seeking to understand we are bringing in empathy too. If we are engaging with our students and their parents with a level of interest and respect for their perspective, we gain trust. Trust and respect come skipping hand-in-hand in the playground of compassion, and are crucial elements in any relationship, no less so in the professional role of teacher.

How to gain trust and respect

We talk of 'earning' respect, which suggests that we need to give something of ourselves to achieve this; it is not something we can assume to have, and it might take some effort. Before we can respect something or someone, we also need a degree of trust. Schools need parents to trust them, in order that they send what is most valuable to them (their children) for their care and education. So how can a school or a teacher earn the respect and trust of parents with whom they have no pre-existing relationship, or repair the damaging assumptions made from previous experiences? The answer is perhaps unexpected, but it is *learning*: in reflecting and communicating the values of a school whereby everybody is interdependent on other members of the school community for learning, teachers-pupils-parents-support staff, and so on. Let's look at two examples of what that means in one comprehensive school:

> 'As head of my department I see myself as a compassionate leader. I have the wisdom to know that my success in my role, is dependent on me learning through my colleagues, my students, their families, the feedback I get, the mistakes that are made, the lessons learnt in experience, we can only grow together if I am eager to learn from those around me, and respect their ideas and opinions.' Ms Jung, Head of Mathematics

> 'As SENDCO, I work closely with our students and their families and really listen to what they tell me they need ... this is what *I* need to learn. This is not always straightforward as a number of the parents I work with also have special needs which might create obstacles to my understanding ... but it is my job to understand, and I take the responsibility for being a compassionate listener, who will try my best to understand and act accordingly.' Mr Patel, Special Educational Needs & Disabilities Coordinator

As we explored in Chapter 2, we often need to be creative about maximising communication opportunities with parents, in order to get our compassionate message across. And just as with that word 'passion' in the middle of 'compassionate', there is nothing more inspiring in leadership than somebody passionate about their job. A sincerely enthusiastic teacher with a passion for learning, who is respectful and compassionate, will always earn trust and respect from pupils, parents and colleagues alike. You've got this. Everything we are promoting within this chapter is really just sharing the love, and stepping up to demonstrate how exciting, interesting, fun, challenging, and engaging learning really is. At this point in the book we'd like you to remind yourselves again of exactly why you went into this job. What was it that sparked that passion for learning and education and what are the skills and gifts you hold in being a great teacher? Teachers tend to be very good at guiding students in highlighting when their behaviours are or are not kind or thoughtful, which is excellent learning for everybody within the classroom setting, and part of the effectiveness of your guidance is that you deliver it from a compassionate mindset. The intelligence of experience, and oversight of the discourse and dialogues within your class, gives you a sociological awareness that the majority of the time, the social or emotional conflicts, upsets or difficulties amongst your pupils are not coming from any evil or bad intent from any one individual towards another. As teachers, you can rationally see what needs to happen in order to defuse tensions, resolve conflict and to restore harmony within your class community. You are in a compassionate mindset, as you know your students, and you know that each individual has a backstory, and is doing the best they can at any given moment with the social intelligence they have and the emotional regulation they are working with as their developing brain matures. You understand people make mistakes, and you encourage your students, that this is all part of learning, and soothe them from any shame they may experience. You see the good in your students. You acknowledge and reward when you see your students being altruistic and empathic, and in all of this, you view your students with a compassionate mindset. What many of us fall short of doing, is extending this compassionate mindset to ourselves. And this is the bit we all must endeavour to work on. It's not a quick fix; we must work hard at extending this compassion to ourselves. Only then can we also view our peers, our colleagues, and all the other adults we come into contact with, directly or indirectly, with the same level of compassion that we all know is what children need to thrive. When we think of this from our rational brain, we know that adults need this too, perhaps we all need it as much as children do. And this is fundamental in our ideology, because in order for the compassionate mindset to be adopted by adults and for adults (as well as children), we need to assume the position of lifelong learners. We need to shift that power that is creating a barrier between the parent-teacher-child triad, by putting compassion at the centre of everything we do.

So now, we must transfer what we already know and do on a daily basis with our students, to self-compassion and working with parents. Let's take a closer look at the compassionate mindset. And as with all our other chapters, we take the focus back to The Self. If empathy is the desire to understand the feelings of others and compassion is the altruistic concern and desire to support the wellbeing of others, we first must know thyself in order to understand how to nurture a compassionate mindset, and the benefits this will have for us, as well as everybody around us. *Nurturing the compassionate mindset* is arguably the best thing you can ever do for your health and wellbeing, and if you take away only one single thing of importance from this book, we hope it is this.

Developing a compassionate mindset

In this section, we'd like to promote the development of a compassionate mindset to optimise your health and wellbeing, and ultimately improve your relationships both professionally and personally.

From the beginning: Our brains

In Chapter 1 we discussed how our brains generate assumptions and rules based on our values and beliefs, and we also explored the emotional impact when rules are broken and assumptions made. In this chapter, we delve a bit deeper into these concepts, so first we must understand how our brain works. The emotional brain is our primitive survival mechanism, it's the oldest part of our evolved brain and is shared by the animal kingdom. It's where all of our emotions arise from: the ones that make us feel good and the ones that don't. Emotions are powerful and each has their own purpose. How we manage these emotions will affect our relationships and our sense of agency and this is the reason, throughout this book, that you are requested to self-reflect. Self-understanding is key, which is why we continue with the theme of working from the inside out. Our emotions are powerful for a reason: they are our messengers and they call us to action. Most of our motivations arise from our emotions whether we are moving away from an emotion we don't want, or towards an emotion that we desire. The brain and all it's programming is incredibly complex and we couldn't possibly go into detail about all the mechanics and wiring, but an overview of its working can be helpful in developing healthy empathy and compassion in order to optimise relationships, and in working with parents.

As we go through life, our brains process and translate all that happens in our world and develop meaning from this. With each interaction and experience a memory is made. If there is a threat attached to that memory, there becomes a direct pathway to the alarm system in the brain. We are hardwired to remember what causes us pain. When we consider physical triggers, this is quite straightforward. For example, we put our hand in the fire and we get burnt, it hurts, we experience physical trauma and emotional shock, we are unlikely to put our hand in the fire again. We might sense varying risk of pain when we feel extreme heat from any source or smell smoke and detect risk of fire. Our brains are constantly picking up unconscious cues, and these keep us alive. Emotional triggers impact on the brain in exactly the same way, and also do so to keep us safe from perceived danger. We are sure we can all think of something that we avoid, due to either an unpleasant associated past experience, or the belief that this thing might trigger fearfulness and uncomfortable emotions; examples might be spiders, driving in the dark or circus clowns. Now, hopefully as teachers, none of you have identified 'being called into school' or 'being summoned to the head teacher's office' as something that evokes fear and trepidation in you. But for many parents, this is absolutely the case. In fact, many parents are extremely uncomfortable just being on school grounds, or having to go through the school gates, for a variety of reasons ranging from social anxiety to traumatic memories of school life and childhood bullying. These feelings evoked by such triggers are not a choice. We react quickly to information, where there is a perceived threat involved, which then triggers a learned response. Like once you've put your hand in the fire, you then learn it's hot, so anything which looks hot in the future you take care and avoid touching it directly. The same with emotional threats. The brain and body remembers every threat, every response and what was effective for getting away and minimising that threat. We may get to a stage where we don't know where that programming came from, that doesn't matter – it's about understanding there is always a reason for any emotional response.

You might be wondering, how on earth is this helpful in working with parents, and how can teachers successfully work with those who are already in a heightened state of arousal just being on school property? This isn't about knowing everyone's story and making allowances for unacceptable behaviour. It's knowing that we don't know anybody else's reality, and accepting that we are all trying to do what we feel is best for ourselves and those that we care for. We are all imperfect and make errors to try and cope with difficult emotions. We cannot possibly understand everyone's story. However, we can work with our own responses to make us authentic and receptive, putting us in the best position to create a space where people feel they can talk openly. And we can train our own brain to develop a compassionate mindset using the following techniques.

Compassionate brain training

1. It is your job to understand all the clues you are being given from the person who is talking to you, with the understanding that the information is not about you, nor your teaching, nor your class, nor the school – the information is all about the speaker. Be curious about your own responses, as you heighten your self-awareness.

2. Remember you are safe. Your compassionate self knows that any emotional responses you are having, are the result of neural programming. You can self soothe by reminding yourself that you are an excellent teacher and learner who cares deeply about other people's life and learning.

3. When you are listening, have awareness of any unconscious emotional responses you might be having to what is being said. These may be physiological feelings such as tension in the muscles, or sudden fatigue, or changes in heart rate or breathing. Keep listening carefully to what is being said and see if you can identify if your emotional responses belong to you, or are in empathy, or over identifying with the person who is talking to you.

4. You are now actively listening, with self-awareness, and checking and regulating your automatic responses, like a pro teaching-learning-compassion-detective, and you didn't even need to say a thing.

5. Find something you really like about the person who is talking to you. Then notice something that you can learn from all the information that they are

giving you. Hold that warm curiosity, and where appropriate and authentic, let the person know the wonderful/helpful/interesting thing you have noticed. If you haven't found anything, ask the person more about what they are saying to you. Sometimes just noting that you can see this parent really wants the best for their child, how important this is and that you want to help – is enough.

6   The more you practise compassionate brain training, the easier it will become, as you manage those automatic responses in healthier ways. At first you may want to practise this particular type of training in private meditation, by bringing to mind the type of dialogue you know triggers the unwanted responses in you, and learning to talk compassionately to yourself in order to self-soothe.

In psychotherapy, this type of technique is sometimes called 'attending to one's inner child'. This might be a helpful way of looking at things for both teachers and parents who find endless compassion for children and their varying needs, but find self-compassion and compassion for other adults more challenging. Don't neglect your inner child. Listen when they whisper 'I'm scared' and also when they are shouting out 'let me out to play!'. Once you can really tune into that voice, you'll find that your stress levels are massively reduced.

The infectious nature of stress reduction

CALM – Compassion Affirmed Learning Motivation

Now, isn't this a pandemic the world needs right now? But it is so true just how infectious it is, when just one person, in any system or structure, starts to imbed a compassionate mindset in the way that they choose to function. We have all seen the negative impacts possible if one person in any social grouping, be it a couple, or a company, becomes excessively stressed, and how that can play out on the relationship, or systems or structure, snowballing into a horribly toxic environment where nobody can function effectively cognitively, emotionally, physically, nor at any level. The converse is indeed true if just one person, in even the most stressful of environments, practises self-compassion, and chooses a compassionate mindset. The capacity for mental growth, spiritual learning, and the affirmation of the associated feel-good emotions, are a natural motivator to keep self-nurturing. An increase in dopamine and a decrease in cortisol, create a powerful chemical shift that is undoubtedly going to improve the general health and wellbeing of anybody feeling prone to stress. And in case you hadn't noticed, teaching comes with many-a-stress. This is always going to be the case and it is the nature of the vocation, but we can choose how we respond to those stressors and you can start practising that right now.

Troubleshooting

Let's go back to empathy, because when discussing this book with colleagues, what came up was that there were themes that recurred with families who just did not seem to make reasonable demands on teachers and schools. How does one empathise when there seems there is no sensible common ground?

As we noted in Chapter 1, we often automatically listen from our own perspective. When we say to somebody 'I know how you feel', do we know how that person really feels, or do we know how we might feel if we were in their situation? This is the subtle but crucial difference. How many times have you heard or has someone said to you, 'I know how you feel', and what has been your reaction to this? It would probably depend on who that person was and your circumstances and relationship. We make an assumption that we know how another person feels because we know how we might feel. There's also the extension to this, where we make an assumption on the feelings, thoughts, motivations or values behind another person's behaviour, based on our own thinking. These factors create blockages to empathic feelings, and when we lack empathy for others, we lack the ability to understand from their perspective and we are more likely to make unhelpful judgements.

Reflect back on what your opinions were on Mrs Brown's morning connections from Chapter 1. What assumptions or judgements did you make?

Let's look at Mr Lemon who had a driving ban for drink-driving. What are your thoughts on that? We are going to assume there are a few judgements being made about Mr Lemon, his behaviour and his values. All we know at this point is he got caught driving over the legal limit. What would your thoughts be if we explained Mr Lemon was caught the morning after his mother's wake? Sometimes we need to be asking for more and more information, more clues as to what is really going on, something for us to work with.

When we talk about empathy, most people have the ability to understand what others are feeling from their own perspective, as opposed to the perspective of the other. This assumption can have a huge impact upon relationships. If we assume we know what someone else is feeling, that assumption erases the curiosity and desire to truly understand. Even if we have experienced and been through the same situation as the other person we claim to have empathy for, it is unhelpful to assume we know what they are feeling. Most of the time we don't know, and as with what we have learnt in the previous two chapters, the best thing we can do is to be aware of this fact, in order that we can tune into the story of the person we are communicating with. Again, in doing so, we take ownership of the responsibility to really understand the perspectives of our fellow beings, and doing so from a loving and compassionate place.

Conclusion

Neuroscience has proven that empathy can be taught, to absolutely anybody, so we have every faith that the readers in this book shall gain expertise faster than most. A compassionate mindset is not only having empathy for others, but also holding compassion and kindness for ourselves. When we are able to take a compassionate perspective, we reduce our stress levels and put ourselves in the optimal position to make meaningful and effective connections with others. Compassion is necessary for forming and maintaining any relationship we encounter, be that personal or professional.

Resources

Student resources

There are so many brilliant resources on compassion out there, and many lists of children's books across the key stages, which we shall include on our website in connection to this book. Below are a few of our favourites.

KS1

Listening with My Heart by Gabi Garcia

KS2

Sam the Magic Genie by Brian Mayne

KS3/4

Mindset by Dr Carol S. Dweck
Positively Teenage by Nicola Morgan
Film – *The Blind Side*, 2009

Teacher and parent resources

Here are some resources for teachers and parents. We have listed these together, as all the resources are suitable and beneficial for adults, generally, and not specific to teaching.

The Compassionate Mind by Paul Gilbert

The Gifts of Imperfection by Brene Brown

Daring Greatly by Brene Brown

Finding Peace in a Frantic World by Penman and Williams

Help the Helper by Babette Rothschild

The Chimp Paradox by Steve Peters www.compassiongames.org/ (accessed 13 October 2021)

Radical Compassion by Tara Brach

Parent Yourself Again by Yong Kang Chan

Self-compassion for Parents by Susan M. Pollak

Mindful Compassion by Paul Gilbert and Choden

Deepak Chopra is also brilliant on this topic and has lots of free resources on YouTube, as well as teaching available on rewiring the brain with compassion, joy and love.

References

Covey, S.R. (1999) *7 Habits of Highly Effective Families*. New York: Simon & Schuster.

4

COMMUNITY

---------------------------- Chapter objectives ----------------------------

- To understand how to develop compassionate communities
- To reflect on community spirit
- To explore and understand psychological health and safety needs
- To consider exercises for developing family relationships
- To examine resources and networking within the wider community.

Introduction

This chapter looks further at how we can build on what we've learned in the previous chapters to develop compassion and connection within the school community in order to strengthen relationships with families connected to your school. The benefits of cultivating this community will be in producing a connected optimal environment and for all those within this environment to have the best possible life chances. Furthermore, enabling members of your school community to be more effective problem solvers with higher levels of resilience will make the community much more effective at responding and managing in times of hardship. The benefit of understanding the components of our value based connections model is that this is all part of a process to make connection. Connection can only develop through openness, and openness can only be cultivated when someone feels safe. If individuals don't feel safe, they are in threat mode which will create thoughts and behaviours which are reactive and defensive.

So, what does community spirit mean to you, and do you have any lived experience of community spirit in action? Post pandemic, many of us will have some ideas of supporting our neighbours, and clapping the National Health Service, and perhaps a feeling of togetherness and camaraderie in times of world crisis. At the time of writing, the world is still adjusting to a new normal, and society has changed forever. We cannot ignore what this means for our communities, and the impact on schools and, no less, teachers. It would be fair to say that teachers have been key to holding society together over the most challenging of circumstances in 2020 and 2021. As we all know, the job of a teacher is about far more than covering curriculum; a teacher's many roles are multi-faceted, and they extend beyond the classroom to the family home and further in to the community. As authors, it is our firm belief that society does not hold up enough recognition for exactly what teachers do, and this is certainly reflected in the salary. Teaching can indeed, at times, feel like a thankless task and it is hard to maintain a compassionate mindset if the feeling is that for all that you are offering, far beyond the call of duty, is being undervalued. So, in this chapter we want to address that, and support you in ways that honour you for the amazing job you are doing – and recognise just how important you are in developing communities to shape a brighter future.

Community spirit

In previous chapters we have worked on developing values, beliefs, communication and compassion, which are the necessary foundation on which we can build a compassionate community. Let's consider Maslow's hierarchy of needs, as they apply to us in our school communities. In Figure 4.1 you'll see our tree-shaped version with those essential basic needs at the root.

As teachers, we are always striving to get right to the top of that tree and allow our students to achieve their full potential. Collectively, we want to share in the joy of that success with our colleagues and our wider school community. However, when you think about your class, or your colleagues, how often are students and/or staff arriving at school with deprivation at their very basic level of needs? How, as teachers, can we be expected to meet these self-fulfilment needs, when it is often outside our control to work with domestic health and safety needs? The answer is in activating the school community, and we will now provide some practical means of doing so.

Exercise 4.1

Personal needs

Working from the inside out, first you must consider your own needs. We invite you to use the hierarchy of needs tree in Figure 4.1, and working from the roots to the top, consider how well your own needs are being met, before taking some time to think about what you need to be higher functioning. There may be things you can do to help yourself, for example, getting more sleep, setting better boundaries

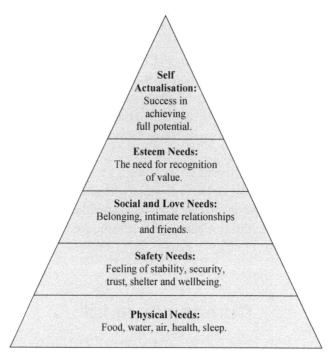

Figure 4.1 Maslow's Hierarchy of Needs Tree

around home and work life, or making certain relationships higher priority in your time. There may also be things that others within your school staff community could do to support you, such as peer supervision, organisational tasks that you might be able to delegate, or specialist resources that could be shared. There are also many ways that families and the wider school community can help. It is well worth spending some time networking with, and getting to grips with local authority support organisations as well as independent charities and voluntary support groups that are operational within your area. Often it is parents that will be able to link you in with projects and initiatives known to them within the community. We have listed some of the national organisations that support young people and families in various ways in our resource section at the end of this chapter. Don't be afraid to reach out and network, because we won't get to the top of our tree on our own. In David Attenborough's witness statement, based on his 93 years of observing the natural world, he reiterates this point: for any environment to thrive, every part of the ecosystem must thrive (2020). In a global sense, we cannot thrive as human beings without taking care of all living things around us. If we do not work collectively and wisely in our communities, society degenerates. We all have our part to play, and teachers have a fantastic opportunity to be right at the centre of the community. From this position, the wise teacher can consider their own needs, and those of their class, and then consider the strengths and skills of other adults around them and how those assets might be best utilised in order that the community meets their needs, and flourishes.

Exercise 4.2

Your team

Now we'd like you to consider your feeling of connectedness towards your peers and colleagues. Are you able to engage openly, being receptive and supportive of one another? If not, it is worth considering the barriers in the way of meaningful connection. In order to develop our community, we need to identify the needs of all members. If there are disparities or lack of unity amongst your staff team, it is far harder to model effective team work, to your students and their families.

Your school community

Let's think now about the health and wellbeing of our school community. The social needs of each school will be different. There may be a high prevalence of specific issues or themes which consume a lot of staff time and resources. Working out how to collectively address these issues will serve each individual belonging to the school community, regardless of whether they are directly affected by the specific issue or not. There is a certain mindset that needs to be adopted in order to, quite literally, buy-into this way of community thinking. Some families' needs are going to be far greater than others. In a community, we should not see that as coming at a cost to others, or a sacrifice or burden to the other community members trying to meet those needs; rather we should regard what we do in meeting the needs of others as an investment in our community. It can be helpful to think of how a family would feel, if they had to pay a lot of money for a life saving operation for one poorly child, the other family members would not resent the loss of a holiday, or even a home to meet the need of their loved one. The family health and togetherness is of utmost importance, and so it should be when we consider the health of our communities. We must listen out for the needs of all members within our communities and collectively support where we can, for the greater good.

Now let's talk about parents ...

Check-out how your families feel in terms of their connection and belonging to the school community. This can be done using regular online surveys, as well as at other contact times and during class. Think about the sub-communities that exist within your wider school community, considering different cultural or religious groups, and any features that create a social group identity such as 'military families', or 'hockey mums'. Think about how people connect and by what means. It can be hard to spot if somebody is feeling isolated, or is going hungry, or suffering in any way, based on social media interactions, or a five-minute chat on school drop. So, it's important that teachers have a strategy for checking in with parents and families. This provides the opportunity to actively involve and include families within school life or to link up the appropriate support agency where needed. Some parents may have no time nor inclination to be any more involved than they already are with school. However, the importance is in them having a sense of belonging in the school community and in school, enabling families to access education through supporting community health and wellbeing.

Breeding a community culture

The compassionate community has to cascade from peer to peer, modelled and ingrained in values and policy that everyone signs up to and lives by. However, we do not live in a perfect world. So let's consider some strategies when working with the realities of creating this culture.

Historically, parenting classes are only offered when a problem is identified that requires intervention from agencies such as social services or young offender's schemes. In fact, much of the time, participation in parenting programmes is part of a court order. This is a sad situation, as there is no support or guidance out there in raising children beyond the preschool years, and very little on adolescents or teenagers, which is a time where parents are less likely to be in regular contact with others as their children become more independent and most parents are then in full time work. So it can be a very isolating experience, being the mum or dad, and none of us have the guide book – it does not exist. Having worked in organisations that provide parenting classes and support, it has always been said amongst staff delivering these programmes, that it would be lovely if all families could take part in these classes – as they are such enriching experiences. Perhaps your school already provides some programmes for selected families, such as Triple P (Positive Parenting Programme). Our suggestion is that as a class teacher, you could provide some of the exercises typically used in these courses, either as home learning or as an evening event at school, as part of Personal, Social, Health and Economic Education. They are all designed for one parent to be working one-to-one with one child. Often, what we find is that if there are siblings in the family, that the parent will take turns at working on the exercises with each child – because it is enjoyable, and great for bonding. Ideally, if you are able to run as a group of parent-child pairs at your school, you shall find that your families start to associate school with nurturing the family, and there you have an inspired and thriving community.

Living with parents' exercises

These can be run as separate exercises or all together for a day/evening event. It is an especially lovely experience if you are able to provide a buffet meal or activity such as roasting marshmallows around an open fire for participants to enjoy together as part of an event. Providing a free meal will increase participation too.

Knowing me Knowing you

Give each parent and child the following question sheets to answer for themselves and to answer for the other. The pairs do this separately and then once complete they compare and discuss answers together, a little like the Mr and Mrs game.

....Parent .... Young person

Favourite colour
Outfit I like to wear the most
Where I would like to go on holiday
Favourite dinner
Scared of
Makes me laugh the most
Favourite zoo animal
Love or hate rollercoasters
Would I rather ride a horse, a bike or motorbike?
Favourite season of the year
Something I like the smell of
Do I have an ambition?
Something I'd like our family to do together more
Do I prefer city or countryside?

Team trust

A course is set up, whereby your pairs take it in turns for one to lead the other safely from start to finish, blindfolded, just by giving verbal instructions alone, and no shouting is allowed. The winner is the person who guides in the fastest time to complete the course, and the person who is guided in the fastest time. You could also set more precise instructions, as a home learning exercise, and then ask pairs to record their times to be compared with other student and parent pairs.

Advice please?

Create some age-appropriate case studies of family disagreements. These might be printed out scenarios on paper, or you could make little role play film clips if you wanted to set this as e-learning. The situations should involve conflicts that might arise in households with children of a similar age. The task is that the student and parent give advice on what they think the best thing would be for the characters in the case study to do in order to resolve the conflict. They must address this for all characters in the case study, considering all perspectives. If you are running this as a group, you could have participants sit in a circle whilst you and colleagues role play the scenarios, then apply the advice given by participants to play out the scene. This is a brilliant way of allowing communities to work together on solving social dilemmas.

The Blob Tree Test

Using *The Big Book of Blob Trees* by Pip Wilson and Ian Long (a must have resource for anybody working with children and young people), ask your pairs to individually identify where they think they are on the blob tree test and then to identify where other members of their family are. Once both people have completed this task, then ask them if they would rather be in a different position on the tree. Your pairs' task is then to discuss and support one another in getting to where they want to be on the tree, and where they'd like one another to be. They can then create their own blob tree representing their goal or vision and notice how that feels.

Paper tower building

The classic team builder, with the added element of class competition, as you can ask families trying this at home to photograph their result and take measurements to send to school and be compared against that of other students. Instructions as follows:

You and your team are to make a strong and stable tower that will hold weight and withstand natural forces.

1   You may use only paper and tape
2   You may use paper beams in your design
3   The tower must have a platform at the top
4   You may not tape the tower to a desk, it must be free standing
5   You have ten minutes to complete the task

Ask your student-parent pair to feed back on what each other's strengths were in this team exercise.

Awards ceremony

If you are running this as a group event, you can use your observations throughout the activities to reward the qualities and strengths you see in each individual. This can be celebrated in a certification ceremony at the end of the event.

Taking this forward

These exercises are designed to be fun and enjoyable, and they are all possible to do at home. They also give the opportunity for you to reach out to families that notice any particular issues with running the activities, and based on feedback you could then offer access to support around the specific issues arising. For example, a parent might report that their young person got frustrated, lost their temper and became aggressive during an activity, or vice versa. This would be worth further exploring and potentially arranging anger management through school, or signposting to the family GP to have some medical or psychological support set up around this. It can be daunting for teachers to become involved with families at this deeper level, and fear can prevent creative problem solving. It is important to remember that there are so many routes you can signpost towards, it's just that very often you are going to be the adult that is first aware of any issues going on for your student's family. That doesn't mean that you are then responsible for solving any problems you uncover, and it can be difficult at times not to feel burdened with information. Your school safeguarding policies and procedures are in place so that you can safely report and know that you have made the appropriate link between school and home. However, let's take a closer look at this matter – because, actually, how your personal and professional needs are met when managing challenging psycho-social matters, is incredibly important for your health and longevity in the job.

As professionals with long careers in working with young people and families, we appreciate that it often doesn't feel as simple as being made aware of an issue, making an appropriate referral or passing on to your head of year, and then relaxing in the knowledge you have done what was required of you. Yes, schools tend to be very well equipped at ensuring the physical safety of staff, students and families is met, with health and safeguarding procedures firmly rooted. However, here we are thinking about emotional safety needs. In order to develop a community that constantly strives to meet the safety needs of every member, we must explore emotional safety for the benefit of all concerned. In Table 4.1 we shall outline some basic emotional safety needs, approaches to meeting those needs, and the purpose and benefits of having those safety needs met. You might like to continue this table from your own experience, and where there are gaps, keep consulting parents, students and colleagues.

Table 4.1 Psychological health and safety

Who does the need belong to?	What is the emotional safety need?	How might this need be met via school (action)?	Purpose and benefit of meeting this need
School staff, students, parents, and wider community.	Connection. Feeling connected to other community members.	School community outreach events such as sports events, stage shows and concerts performed for audiences in the community, inviting families and the wider community into the school, as well as going out to residential care homes to meet people there.	Events such as these give everybody a part to play in supporting one another, and engaging in a positive and enjoyable experience collectively. This is great for raising morale and optimising the opportunity for meaningful connections to be made through common interest.
School staff, students, parents.	Structure. Understanding what is expected within any given role. This might include input or responsibilities.	Clearly communicated guidance around expected or encouraged behaviours and how they relate to the school values.	It is easy for subcultures, or potentially harmful behaviours to creep into any institution. In order for a school to stay strong to its values, the school must be consistently communicating the expectations of/on staff, parents and pupils, in order that all feel secure in the expected standards for themselves and others. This also makes it clearer when to delegate responsibilities.
School staff, students, parents and the wider community.	Care. Feeling valued and cared for by other community members.	Sometimes we have to accept that there are emotional needs unmet that are outwith our control. School cannot replicate or compensate if caring and loving behaviours are lacking in a home environment. However, by talking responsibility to model loving behaviours to all that you come into contact with – you shall demonstrate that way of being.	As we understand, from developing a compassionate mindset, it is very possible to conquer emotional struggles, resolve conflict, and heal wounds from meeting every situation with a loving attitude. It is especially important that we allow children to realise their worth from a young age for healthy development of their sense of self.

(Continued)

Table 4.1 Psychological health and safety (*Continued*)

Who does the need belong to?	What is the emotional safety need?	How might this need be met via school (action)?	Purpose and benefit of meeting this need
School staff, students, parents and the wider community.	Boundaries. The separation of school life and home life; professional and personal; safe limits and parameters.	Timetable self-care into your diary, alongside lesson planning and other aspects of professional preparation and development.	As human beings we play many roles within our lives, and (going back to our hierarchy of needs) rest is a baseline need, in order that we function effectively and don't get ill. Mental exhaustion and compassion fatigue are real issues – and if we don't protect ourselves from over-working, or we find ourselves stressed by work situations, we run into extreme danger for both our mental and physical health and wellbeing.

We are sure there are plenty of mental safety needs you could identify for you and your school community, and we encourage you to do so. It is of utmost importance that you are protected as a teacher and as it stands, the teaching culture is one which rewards overworking and neglect of self care. Statistical evidence shows the very high levels of burn-out amongst teachers of all levels of experience, and as authors, we are passionate at instilling a change to this tragic culture. With no available guidance for good practice from the Department of Education, and the Teaching Regulation Agency being more about what not to do than protecting the health of our teachers – it seems that only the teacher's unions are speaking out about this neglectful oversight. It is a well-known fact, that stress stunts healthy growth and development; it kills creativity, and prohibits passion. So, it is a cruel irony that we are playing into a system that places our masters of learning and stalwarts of community in such a highly stressful position with regard to workload and hours. It is time to make those changes in your own professional life, and we hope this book will support you in doing so.

Conclusion

By encouraging parents, families and the wider community, to engage with school – be that by outreach work, outside of school and within the community, or inviting others in – for sports events, concerts and such like – you will put your school at the heart of a supportive and supported community, where everybody that buys into your school values and ethos is welcome. Teachers are all too often burdened with many responsibilities outside of the curriculum and class teaching. It is important that multi-agency working is coordinated, so that families have specialist support and intervention from professionals outside of school, in order that education is not disrupted, teachers can focus on teaching, and communities can thrive. By considering our needs, from the inside out, examining our individual needs, moving towards our collective needs, we can actively improve our collaborative operation as a community and ultimately improve lives and living.

Resources

Student resources

Again, there is lots of literature at primary school level available for your libraries and listed on our website. Here are some of our favourites.

KS1

All Are Welcome by Alexandra Penfold
Our Class is a Family by Shannon Olsen

KS2

Whose Side Are You On? by Alan Gibbons
Wonder by R.J. Palacio

KS3/KS4

Watch the film 'Pay It Forward' and ask students to set their own individual, family and class goals for how they might positively contribute to community and make a difference.

Another inspirational watch is 'Glasgow Girls'. This is an hour-long musical drama made in 2014, based on the true story of a group of teenagers who fight to save their classmate from deportation. This story shows a school community in action, and at its best.

Literature

Helping Teens Stop Violence, *Build Community* and *Stand for Justice* by Allan Creighton and Paul Kivel
Together is Better by Simon Sinek
The Noughts and Crosses series by Malorie Blackman
The Dark Beneath by Alan Gibbons

Teacher resources

The Mentally Healthy Schools Workbook: Practical Tips, Ideas and Whole-school Strategies for Making Meaningful Change by Pooky Knightsmith
Diversity in Schools by Bennie Kara
A Little Guide for Teachers: Teacher Wellbeing and Self-care by Adrian Bethune and Emma Tell
Psychology for Teachers by Paul Castle and Scott Buckler

Parent resources

Where to Draw the Line by Anne Katherine
Belong by Radha Agrawal
Caught in the Crossfire by Christine Fauconnier
When the Adults Change Everything Changes by Paul Dix

National organisations which support young people and families:

www.accessiblecountryside.org.uk/family-orgs (accessed 13 October 2021); Action for Children; Adfam; Advisory Centre for Education (ACE); Alliance for Inclusive Education (Alfie); Anxiety UK; Barnardo's; Beat Bullying; Care for Family; Child Accident Prevention Trust; Child Bereavement Charity; ChildLine; Child Exploitation and Online Protection Centre (CEOP); Child Poverty Action Group; Circles Network; Combat Stress; Contact a Family; DadTalk; Disabled Parents' Network; DrugFam; Family Action; Family Lives; Fatherhood Institute; Family and Friends of Lesbians and Gays (FFLAG); Gingerbread; Grandparents Plus; Home-start; Hyperactive Children's Support Group; Internet Watch Foundation; Keyring; KIDS; Kidscape; Mosac; Mothers 35 Plus; National Children's Bureau; NCPCC; Parentkind; PAPYRUS; Professional Association for Childcare and Early Years; Rainbow Trust Children's Charity; Rays of Sunshine Children's Charity; Rape Crisis; Reuben's Retreat; Shelter; Single Parent Action Network; Soldiers, Sailors, Airmen and Families Association; The Compassionate Friends; The National Association of Widows; Together Trust; Turning Point; UK Parents' Lounge; UK Safer Internet Centre; We Are with You; WAY foundation.

References

Attenborough, D. (2020) *A Life on Our Planet*. London: Ebury Press.

5

WORKING WITH EMOTIONAL CHALLENGES

———————————— Chapter objectives ————————————

- To consider different types of emotional challenges
- To examine psychological safety in response to case examples
- To introduce Karpman's drama triangle
- To study responses to family crisis
- To examine structuring and running peer supervision sessions.

Introduction

Life is what happens when you're busy lesson planning. Some of what you face, in working with families, will be frequent issues which you have effective policies and procedures to follow in response to the situation (for example, homework policy); others will be things that come by infrequently and there may be little guidance in the way a school should respond in that situation (for example, sudden death of a student's parent). No matter which it is, either the frequent and easily actionable response or the traumatic isolated incident that no-one could have expected, what is necessary, and seems to be very lacking in the procedures for many schools, is prioritising the psychological safety of the staff *as well as students*. Schools tend to be excellent at the latter and psychological safety for students is, quite rightly, a key focus. However, there is very little guidance in this area for teachers and school staff. In this chapter, we will provide you with guidance in order that you feel in the best, and safest, place to respond to the life challenges you meet, within the day-to-day running of your classroom. Staff psychological wellbeing has to be prioritised. We would just like to emphasise at this stage we are covering your emotional responses to difficult situations and not advising on policy or procedures which your school will already have in place.

There are a whole variety of complex needs that can come into the classroom which will require and benefit from family involvement. Everything from mental health issues, learning needs, emotional and behavioural needs, to physical health, psycho-social needs, poverty and family crisis. As professionals, you have the skills and very likely the policy to respond to any of these issues in a practical way. However, your response can be affected by the psychological impact the issue has on you. Furthermore, it is highly likely that disclosure of delicate information from pupils will come at a time where you also have the task of teaching the rest of your class. On all levels it is far from the ideal setting in which you can give the pupil delivering the delicate information, the time, space, safety and confidentiality required at that moment in time (with 30 sets of eyes and ears also in the situation). As well as the issues with the immediacy, we also have the wider restraints in working with families. All teachers are time poor due to the demands of the job, so a family requiring a lot of support can take up time which you don't have to spare. The most emotionally demanding families you may even mentally take home with you and worry about. Each of these situations is going to create varying levels of distress and the following ideas will help you on how to cope and manage that effectively. It is vital that the first components of this book have been explored, as we will start to build on these concepts within the interventions. Let's consider the following scenarios, internal responses, and effective management ensuring psychological safety.

The desk-time disclosure

Manda has gone to her maths teacher's desk as she is stuck with her algebra task. Mrs Acharya asks Manda if she can see what she did in the homework exercise preparing for this particular task. Manda suddenly becomes upset and says that she's not able to do the homework, as she's got to look after her younger siblings. Mrs Acharya notices that Manda looks very tired, and that she appears not to have washed, judging by her body odour and dirty looking uniform. Mrs Acharya feels sad for her, and wonders what is going on at home. However, this is maths class and there are several students also needing help and assistance. How should Mrs Acharya respond?

In the immediacy, a compassionate response will allow Manda to feel that her teacher is not ignoring the wider problem. Mrs Acharya could say, 'Ah, I can see you are upset and worried about not being able to do your homework, let us focus on this now, and we'll figure something out to get you some extra support, if you leave it with me.' If Manda is still displaying emotional upset, Mrs Acharya might not be able to create time in which to offer further response. If it is possible to have another member of staff cover, it would be appropriate to invite Manda to have a further chat about what is upsetting her, in a private area. You may have a school guidance team or it may be your Senior Leadership Team, that have an appointed position for managing pupil wellbeing. It may be you liaise with your safeguarding lead for further guidance. So, on checking out what it is troubling Manda, you might then be able to refer Manda to the appropriate member of staff to help directly with the problems she is having preventing her from doing homework. You can then return to your class.

But what then? You have an awareness that Manda looks and smells neglected. You have managed the situation and done everything in your control to help her appropriately. You now have an awareness that there are pressures at home, and that they are impacting Manda's learning, so you are sensitive to this and try not to single her out to answer questions. You notice that other children don't want to sit near Manda because she smells bad. This is a difficult situation for any teacher to witness. How might Mrs Acharya feel? Perhaps you recall how you have felt in a similar situation to Mrs Acharya, or indeed Manda.

The key to managing psychological safety is in what happens beyond the immediacy, and how this is followed up as a school. For Mrs Acharya to feel supported by her peers, and that she is able to share not only her concerns for the student but also her own emotional responses, appropriately and confidentially, will help Mrs Acharya navigate this situation safely. One way of doing this is using peer supervision – which we have given you guidance for at the end of this chapter.

Having follow-up information about what has been put in place for Manda's family is going to be of great help to Mrs Acharya. One of the great psychological challenges in this whole scenario is the powerlessness that a teacher might feel in the situation. In the first instance the teacher is not expecting any kind of disclosure, particularly one that indicates a requirement for child protection measures. Mentally the teacher is expecting to help the student with the algebraic problem. So, to then be suddenly responding to a potential crisis, is naturally unsettling – and particularly so as a teacher has not got the powers to change the situation nor address what may or may not be going on in the student's family life. Too often, front line professionals are in the position where they can refer onwards, but then have no feedback about what has changed, or what the result of that referral was. So, there is no known resolution nor outcome, leaving the teacher feeling yet more vulnerable as there is no closure on the situation that was in the first instance, trusted in the teacher's hands. It is important that schools do follow-up, and that there is a way of checking exactly what actions have been taken beyond disclosures leading to referrals of this nature. By creating a review process, teachers should be able to look at any such incidents, and consider what was actioned and with what results – identifying lessons for future. This type of review process is active learning for professional development and creates a proactive system which empowers teachers and school staff in generating best practise guidelines. By giving teachers the ability to review the outcomes of their referrals, we also give autonomy. Feeling in control and having the ability to problem solve effectively reduces the enormous levels of stress that are naturally created by the helpless feeling of impotence in meeting a student's needs. We look at this matter again in Chapter 7: Agency.

The emotional incident within class/school time

Caleb and Jacob are 15-year-old twin brothers, who suffer great jealousy of one another, and this has caused a complete breakdown in their sibling relationship. When their parents separate it is decided that Caleb lives with Mum and Grandmother, and Jacob goes to live with Dad and Dad's girlfriend Roxy. Jacob has realised at school that Caleb has started dating Roxy's daughter, Lexi. Jacob is furious and wants an end to this relationship. He tells other students that this is incestuous and that Caleb and Lexi are perverted and weird. Very quickly, as tensions escalate, school staff and the Senior Leadership Team become aware of this problem. What happens next?

In the immediacy, where possible, school guidance or SLT should hold separate one-to-one meetings with Caleb, Jacob and Roxy, to hear their part in the story. It may be that things can be resolved in this way, without any further problems or issues. If this looks unlikely and there is no sense of resolve, what then?

Teachers would be right to feel reluctant about bringing in the parents, as potentially there are then three or four different conflicts going on in the room. However, if the situation is left without intervention, this could result in an escalation of conflict, and even bullying or injury. Schools might also find themselves in a position where the parents show up to school uninvited, given that it is in school and not in the families' homes, that the conflict is taking place. So, it is wise to reduce this risk by contacting all of the parents involved and making individual telephone appointments to speak with them at a time that is mutually convenient.

Issues like this are very delicate and nuanced, and require great skill in handling. It is very often the case that schools simply do not have the capacity to do so, and if no reasonable way forward can be found with what school can offer, counselling should be sought, and mediation for the families. There is a limit to what can be expected of teachers and if at SLT level it is decided this case is for external referral, it would then be fair to make other staff working with the young people concerned aware of the situation. Then, appointed staff members can make regular check-ins with the young people concerned to assess how things are going.

It is not appropriate to ask counsellors about their work with clients, as this is confidential; you may, however, have a three way agreement in order that you can check-in with progress and for any recommendations of how school might support, such as delivering emotional resilience packages. We are assuming that your schools have got their own age appropriate programmes and strategies in supporting psychological safety for students, but please see our resource section in the previous chapter to access relevant training and/or further support.

Families with close school and ongoing social services involvement

The McGuiness family and the Razer family have several children at Farmfun Primary School. Both families are known to social services as well as housing, the police and the prison service. There are ongoing and regular reviews for the support of each of the children belonging to these families and they have various support channels in place including charities such as Barnardo's, Action for Children, and Action for Prisoners' Families. The children are all progressing and developing as desired under their individual plans, and there have been no behavioural or emotional incidents that the staff at Farmfun Primary did not feel more than able to deal with at school. However, the adult members of these families are constantly feuding and often bring those issues to the SLT. There have been times that the McGuiness family have refused to send their children to school as they've been unhappy that school had not chastised the Razer parents for some matter or other. These families take up a disproportionate amount of staff time at all levels.

Some families will have a large number of professionals from many different agencies working alongside them. The best strategy for schools in working with these families is calling a multi-agency meeting of all professionals involved, to meet at school, in order that school can chair then delegate responsibilities accordingly – ideally with the family in attendance. That way, everybody has a document of actions, including the family and all school staff and this can be referred to when approached by the families. It is then also possible for messages to be taken and noted to take to the future reviews or passed to the relevant teams. Again, it is important that class teachers have awareness of what is happening behind the scenes in order that they can not only reassure a child of what support they can expect, but also feel reassured themselves and psychologically safe from the burden of tasks beyond a school's reach.

Vulnerable families

Taylor is a 6-year-old who is sometimes with a foster family, as Taylor's birth mum is having cancer treatment and Taylor's birth father struggles with Borderline Personality

Disorder and Chronic Fatigue. Taylor experiences gender dysphoria and so the school has agreed to use the preferred name 'Taylor' and gender neutral pronouns as Taylor prefers to be viewed as 'not a boy and not a girl'. Other children are fine with this; however, many adults forget to use Taylor's chosen name, and neutral pronouns and this causes Taylor distress. Taylor's class teacher, Mr Chen, finds the whole family situation 'heartbreaking' and he can't help but try to compensate in his kindness towards Taylor, for what is such a tragic situation. Mr Chen has also read *Lessons in Love and Understanding*, so has familiarised himself with making school a safe place for Taylor to express their gender identity, as well as talk about their unique family structure. So, how does Mr Chen protect himself from feeling overwhelmed with his feelings of sorrow and sympathy? How can Mr Chen stay psychologically safe?

Firstly, as professionals working with children we must be clear about our own boundaries (more about this in Chapter 6) and be aware that children are very tightly bonded, and have deeply meaningful relationships with their families – whether they are with birth parents, guardians, carers or other parental figures. We are not in that role. Roald Dahl's *Matilda* gives us the perfect example of the charitable teacher, Miss Honey, a vulnerable child once herself, rescuing Matilda from the shambolic parenting and neglect of her ignorant parents (and let's not even go there with Miss Trunchbull's headship). As caring and compassionate beings who are experts in meeting the needs of children, the temptation for teachers to 'rescue' is huge when we work with vulnerable families. However, this is actually an ineffective way of supporting anybody. If we consider Karpman's Drama Triangle (Figure 5.1), we can see the interplay and exchanges that take place between the triad of parent-teacher-child and the positions we then create when our rescuer response elicits a persecutor and a victim.

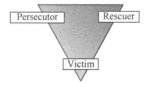

Figure 5.1 Karpman's Drama Triangle

Reproduced with kind permission of Stephen B. Karpman, M.D.

Karpman's Drama Triangle can be used to look at the different roles we might play out in any type of conflict scenario. In the example of Mr Chen making himself 'rescuer' of Taylor, Taylor becomes 'victim', which puts the family in the role of 'persecutor'. From the information we have, Taylor's family life may be going along very well. The combination of a loving foster family, with birth parents who are doing their best by their child in challenging circumstances, may be just what Taylor needs. Using the drama triangle we can also see how other possibilities in the same triad might play out. We might have Taylor's family taking the victim position, and feeling with all that is going on for them that Mr Chen being too much of a soft-touch, was not supporting them in their combined efforts to raise Taylor with appropriate boundaries and discipline. Mr Chen has become persecutor, and Taylor is then in the position of rescuer – as Taylor really doesn't want his family nor teacher to feel bad, so must try and help them solve this misunderstanding. Finally, let's put Taylor as the persecutor, as their emotional needs, amongst all the other demands of Mr Chen's time, are overwhelming and Mr Chen becomes Victim, feeling he cannot possibly cope with all that is expected of him as a teacher. Taylor's family rescues this situation in trying to reassure Mr Chen that everything is really OK, and that Taylor needs boundaries and structure, like all the other children in class, and that it's better just to treat Taylor the same as the other pupils.

When examining any type of conflict situation, it can be helpful to look at Karpman's Drama Triangle in considering the roles that we play out. It is possible for one person to play several roles, even within one conversation, and there isn't a judgement about the roles we play. What is interesting to observe is the position our responses come from – and the position they evoke in the other person/people. Sometimes a response can change the initial position in dialogue, for example, a parent going in to make a complaint to school about their child being bullied might do so as rescuer, with the child as victim and the school/teacher/bully as persecutor. The teacher has more information about this situation and is upset about the way the parent has approached the school. The teacher becomes 'victim', the parent now 'persecutor', the children involved need to be honest and give information to rescue this situation. Again, this is all about self-awareness and having the ability to view situations with a compassionate mindset, to enable effective problem solving.

Family crisis

Headteacher, Miss Bello, has arrived in her office early on Monday morning, to discover that the father of three students attending her school, has been killed in a road traffic accident at the weekend. Miss Bello has an email from the children's widowed mother, stating that the children will be in school as usual, and requesting that the teachers don't talk about the accident in order that the children can be in school 'as normal'. This is a very difficult and shocking email for Miss Bello to receive, and she puts out an urgent notice to all school staff to attend a crisis meeting at 8am, or to report to her office as soon as they arrive at school for their next duties. Miss Bello then attempts to call the grieving parent, to offer condolences and have a fuller discussion about how to best support the family.

At some stage in every teacher's career, there is the point of having a student who is in the raw grief of bereavement, or has suffered a traumatic event. Some children live in daily crisis, for example where there is domestic violence in the family home. In all matters of PSHE, we must teach with the assumption that there are people in the room affected by the matters that we cover. Much of this might be private matters that we shall never know, and of course, some information we shall be privy to, such as in Miss Bello's case.

It is a natural response for adults to believe that they are in some way shielding children from pain by not talking about difficult subjects, or by pretending something hasn't happened, with the hope that children will feel comforted by 'not being reminded' of something painful affecting their lives. In fact, this strategy is not psychologically safe. Denial and false pretence do not allow us to process difficult information and emotions, and the traditional British culture of 'stiff upper lip' along with the more modern tendency to put a positive spin on all that we experience, can really end us all in an unmanageable muddle. In the example with Miss Bello, she does exactly the right thing to reach out to the family. She may, of course, not be able to immediately reach the grieving mum when she tries to call. However, when she does establish contact, it will be helpful for Miss Bello to explain that school would like to acknowledge the family's grief and offer the children any support they can to meet their individual needs at this time. As a teacher, it is always helpful to know exactly what school and the local area can offer in terms of support and your SLT will be able to advise you on this. There are also many ways to demonstrate that you care about how your student feels, without necessarily opening the topic of conversation directly. Making time to discreetly enquire how your pupil is feeling, and offering to be a friendly ear if they need a chat during break time, can go a long way. Having worked with many bereaved clients, we have rarely heard anybody say they were upset because somebody said the wrong thing to them in offering condolences, but commonly it is noted when people avoid the bereaved, or act like nothing has happened.

Coping with distress

It might be that there are particular issues that deeply resonate with you as an individual, and it can be hard to keep safe when you are dealing with your own psychological stuff whilst trying to support another family. The skill of self-awareness is going to be key here for psychological safety. If you are faced with a situation that you find distressing there has to be a level of personal responsibility. A situation such as a tragic incident within a family would be more profound for the individual learning of this tragic situation if they had experienced this specific tragedy within their own history. The information is processed differently and can be extremely distressing and traumatic. There may also be incidents whereby having been informed of something incredibly difficult and distressing, you then have to go and teach a class. In this situation you have no choice, but it's important that there is an effective system in place so staff feel they are able to seek appropriate support. Psychological safety means working on being self aware, open and receptive for students and their families and for your colleagues as well. If you are not already aware of how to seek support for you or your colleagues, please enquire about counselling therapy provision for your school staff. In England, there are NHS talking therapies which can be accessed locally. School staff employed by local authorities should have confidential access via self-referral for free or subsidised counselling services. It is highly advisable to use these sessions should you find yourself affected by any issues that come up for families or others at work. Not only will it keep you psychologically safe, to do so – but it will also improve your wellbeing, increase your self-awareness and support your professional development in teaching.

How to structure and run peer supervision sessions

Peer supervision is an excellent way of keeping teachers and school staff psychologically safe. There are different ways to structure this and you can arrange it to suit the needs of your group, taking into consideration time constraints. There is also no need to have every group member there (so if only two out of seven of you can make it one week, that's fine). Normally, in a place of work, you might have an email group and appoint two or three people to bring a situation to the group and rotate for each session. Each individual has time to present their case. It can be something they found awkward or emotionally challenging in relation to working with a student, an ethical dilemma, or a scenario that played out that they'd like different viewpoints on, or anything they'd like to bring, including success stories to share. The person presenting then asks the group for the feedback, advice, opinions or support they would like. This is not a space for criticism and should be a supportive place where everybody can learn from the sharing of experience in a confidential and professional way. It can be helpful to have a group participant who is not presenting, to facilitate and keep time, as sometimes scenarios involve lots of background and detail that can take too long and may not all be relevant. Of course, the usual codes of confidentiality apply, and teachers must only share names and other details of their students and student's families on a need-to-know basis. For group-supervision purposes, it is rarely necessary to name children at all, as it is focused on the practice of the professional. Group supervision is not a place for safeguarding cases. However, should a case be brought to group-supervision that is deemed to be so, then discussion must be discontinued immediately and the case should go through the appropriate safeguarding procedures. As with any group of this nature, you contract at the beginning of each session for your agreed rules (which might change according to who attends each group).

Immediately at the beginning and directly at the end of each group-supervision session, a grounding exercise is a therapeutic way of bringing focus mindfully to the present (at the start) and disrobing from the process (at the end) and be prepared to step back out of the group, free of burden and distraction. Some groups choose to do one or other, and also have a check-in or check-out, whereby each group member says a little about how they are feeling either going into the session, or on leaving the session. Learning and taking turns to lead grounding exercises is a fantastic transferable skill that can be used in all group settings. Perfect for the classroom. You can be creative with this, using movement, meditation, reflective poetry or prose, guided visualisation, mindfulness – and you can raise energy or create calm based on a sense of what the group need at any time.

Sample script

(Group of five teachers arrive from end of day administrative tasks, pull chairs into a circle and make themselves comfortable with water or coffee to hand. Pre-arranged by email, five of eight teachers are able to attend. They have self-nominated T2 and T3 are going to present and T1 shall facilitate this week. The group have 60 minutes and the facilitator shall keep to time so both T2 and T3 have a fair chance for their presentation, questions to the group and responses.)

T1: Welcome everybody. I'd like to invite you to join me for a grounding exercise to start the session. If we can start on our feet and have a good shake out of all the stresses and strains of the day, shaking our hands, arms, heads, bodies, legs, feet and feeling a sense of any negativity leaving our bodies. Now if I can ask you to sit comfortably, with both feet rooted to the floor, arms relaxed, I am going to talk you through a mindful body-scan visualisation. (Continues maximum of five minutes.) Now gently bringing your attention back to the room, becoming aware of your feet still rooted to the floor, is there anything anybody would like to share with the group, before we have the first presentation?

T5: Thank you, I would just like to share that my dog died this morning, and I'm feeling very sad having had to hold-it-together all day, so I may appear more emotional than usual today, and that's why.

(T1-4 all offer condolences)

T1: Is there anything you need from the group to feel supported right now?

T5: No, thank you, it's kind of you all to care and I feel better having told you.

T4: Does anybody mind if I eat during this session, as I'm feeling very hungry?

   (all other teachers agree that the group should eat and drink as to feel comfortable)

T1: OK, well if T2 or T3 would like to pick who starts, can we hear the first presentation please, and I'll keep you to time so we can have questions and support before moving on to the next presentation.

(presentations and questions to group, support, feedback and conversation from group)

T1: OK, everybody, we are coming to the end of our session and I'd just like to check is everybody satisfied with what we have covered in our discussion today?

(all say they are happy)

T1: As we are just about at time, could I ask that we go around the group and check out using three words that describe how you are feeling right now?

T2: Relieved, supported, encouraged.

T3: Happy, motivated, inspired.

T4: Thoughtful, insightful, excited.

T5: Exhausted, sad, supported.

T1: Grateful, appreciative, honoured (leaves silence for reflective space). Thank you everybody. Can we agree a time, date and facilitator for the next meeting?

T3: I'm happy to facilitate. Is two weeks' time OK to give the others a chance of making it rather than waiting a month, and I'll email out to see who would like to present a case?

(other teachers agree this is fine)

T1: Perfect. Thank you everybody. Feel free to do as you need to do now before you leave this space. Go well, take care and well done us for excellent work, team.

Creating a culture where people feel secure in asking for support and accepting it as well as feeling empowered in the knowledge of where they may be able to offer support to others, is not an easy thing to do within school communities. However, by adopting processes such as group supervision, you can actively influence this culture, and see the benefits in emotional wellbeing and psychological safety, for all involved directly and indirectly.

Conclusion

There are endless possibilities as to the different types of emotional challenges that will impact us throughout our lives and careers. Working closely with children and young people, we are actively seeking to create a psychologically safe environment in our schools and classrooms. However, in doing so, we must also protect our own psychological safety. Our hope is that by working through our case examples, and adopting strategies for psychologically safe responses to emotional challenges, that you might feel better prepared and equipped, come what may, in working with families.

Resources

Student resources

We have to be careful around the resources we suggest to be used in schools. This is because many of the 'draw and talk' type of packages should be part of a therapeutic intervention, rather than what happens in lessons or in response to psychological distress. The books below are all about helping young people to connect with their emotions in a healthy way.

KS1

Let's Talk About Feelings – Usbourne book collection

KS2

The Feelings Book by Lynda Madison

KS3/4

The 7 Habits of Highly Effective Teens by Sean Covey
Embracing the Awkward by Joshua Rodriguez
Dad's Great Advice for Teens by Marc Fienberg
www.youngminds.org.uk (accessed 14 October 2021)
The Mental Elf on Twitter

Teacher resources

The Healthy Coping Colouring Book and Journal by Pooky Knightsmith (can be used across key stages as teacher feels appropriate)
Help for the Helper by Babette Rothschild
Understanding, Nurturing and Working Effectively with Vulnerable Children in Schools: 'Why can't you hear me?' by Angela Greenwood
Lessons in Love & Understanding: Relationships, Sexuality and Gender in the Classroom by Jenni Gates and Scott Buckler
www.youngminds.org.uk (accessed 14 October 2021)

Parent resources

The Book You Wish Your Parents Had Read (and your children will be glad that you did) by Philippa Perry
The Whole-brain Child: 12 Proven Strategies to Nurture Your Child's Developing Mind by Daniel J. Siegal
Anything by Daniel J. Siegal is brilliant in terms of understanding more about the developing brain and the impact on behaviours and emotions – he has lots of talks on YouTube that we would recommend looking up. *Parenting from the Inside Out* is another great title for your parent's lending library.
Parenting the New Teen in the Age of Anxiety by John Duffy
The Highly Sensitive Person and *The Highly Sensitive Child* by Elaine Aron

6

SUPPORTING FAMILIES WITH SEND

—————————— Chapter objectives ——————————

- To introduce SEND families
- To consider expectations, limitations and boundaries
- To examine mental health and psychological safety
- To reflect on case examples and responses
- To consider specific resources for SEND safeguarding and care from the inside out
- To reflect on behavioural responses of parents and families.

Introduction

At this stage in the book, we have worked through the ways in which we make meaningful connections, communicate and work as compassionate communities, teaching and learning through the emotional rollercoaster of life. Having considered all of this, we are going to take a closer look at working with families specifically who have special needs and disability. Now, as all experienced teachers know, this is not as simple as looking at the Educational Health Care Plan that comes neatly packaged along with the student arriving in our class for the first time. Part of the detective work that comes with being a great teacher is figuring out when there is neurodiversity, additional or special needs and how best to meet those needs. These may not be academic, cognitive or physical needs; we are regularly working with psycho-social, emotional and mental health needs, and often a combination of several of these. Of course, this extends to families and teachers too, not just your students. It may be that you have a student who has care responsibilities for a parent with special needs, so the student's needs are vicarious. There are also many adults who live with but never receive a diagnosis for needs such as autistic spectrum conditions and sensory processing disorders.

Whatever the situation, it is always helpful to have a picture of the family system that your pupils gain the other part of their education within: their home life.

Expectations, limitations and boundaries

Previously we explored where our expectations come from, as teachers and human beings. The expectations families have of teachers will vary. Often it is unmet expectations that can create a lot of distress for teachers and families alike. This can then cause difficult inter-actions between school and families. This is why we must be demonstrative in our values from the beginning, be very clear on what schools need to fulfil by law, and have well-set boundaries which are effectively communicated. Teachers will have ideas and expectations of parents and they too need to be able to manage their response if those expectations aren't met. Unless there is a clear safeguarding issue requiring intervention from an out of school support agency, there can be very little teachers can do, even if you feel a family's home life is detrimental to a child's wellbeing. This is one such example when the psycho-logical safety of teachers needs to be discussed and managed: when concerns for a child are distressing, whether or not this is a safeguarding level case.

As mental health professionals, one of the most common difficulties we see for teach-ers or school staff working with SEND/Neurodiverse families is in the common condi-tion we shall refer to as 'professionals having a flap'. In the therapy room, we know that actually, everybody has the best intentions at heart, and wants the best for each and every student. However, in the stress of real life and the various challenges and demands faced by teachers and parents alike (albeit that those challenges can be vastly different at home/in school), effective communication can be lost to the level that it overwhelms and reduces the capacity of the professional to manage, and effectiveness in reaching the needs of the family is impaired. This is not due to lack of competence, empathy, skill, or any such predicament. It is the impact of a system that lands responsibility of an unrealistic, and psychologically dangerous, level of burden on the teacher. Parents and teachers also may set unrealistic expectations upon themselves, underpinned by a belief that they have the responsibility to fix the situation. This perfect storm typically doesn't end well for anyone, but it's likely to leave everyone involved feeling wounded, resulting in damaged relationships and challenging future communication and connec-tions on all sides. We aim to help instigate change here.

SEND and mental health

We have spoken about emotional need and mental health in a general context, but let's closely consider what this means for any of our families with SEND and neurodiversity. Sometimes it's easy to get bogged down in EHCP and our expectations of the student when actually what we must pay most attention to is the 'here and now' in our classroom.

Exercise 6.1

Psychological barriers to education

We invite you to consider, on any given day and lesson, the emotional and mental health barriers to education in your classroom. As you consider the possibilities for your families, start to also compile a list for the adults in your classroom or school staff community.

This can become an overwhelming exercise once we start, as the possibilities are endless and complex when we consider children that have recognised needs (either through psychology or our own observations). So what is it that we can do to make our classrooms an environment conducive to learning, taking all of this into consideration, and the wellbeing of our whole school community?

Firstly, what not to do. As mental health professionals, the use of interventions such as Thrive techniques, concerns us. These therapeutic techniques are only safe when the practitioner is able to work with what comes up in the sessions. This is not the role nor responsibility of a teacher and nor should it be. With CAMHS waiting lists as they are, there needs to be clear boundaries in place to protect the teacher from 'picking up' where supporting agencies are overwhelmed and absent in appropriate response. We can appreciate that having recognised SEND that it's not always a straight forward referral for diagnosis and support, and therefore please see resources section in Chapter 5 for agencies which can offer advocacy and guidance.

Once we have identified relevant resources and services to collaborate with, we can then focus on our class and our students. This is an interesting phenomenon in itself as most teachers will experience in their career a time where they feel the needs of individual students take their attentions away from the rest of the class, and focus is concentrated on certain students sometimes with SEND or whose families believe there to be a SEND concern that needs attention. What you can safely utilise are the therapeutic tools that counsellors and psychotherapists use systemically with groups in order to work with your whole class at the same time as addressing any particular needs of individuals that emerge in this process.

Other techniques that are used by schools are body work sessions such as applied yoga and massage for SEND pupils, using Pupil Premium (PP) funds to bring in qualified practitioners for group and individual work. Being in a classroom full of stimuli and stressors is hard work and takes a lot from SEND students. Working with the body and giving something back, in terms of energy and relief from stress, can be massively beneficial.

Inside-out thinking

Let's first reframe our thinking. We are *not* trying to attempt to make students and families fit into the criteria of a pre-existing school system. We are sure most teachers did not go into the profession with this type of one-size-fits-all approach in mind. Rather, as professionals, we are best when we have the support structure that allows for creative teaching, within the incredible diversity we experience in each and every place of education: isn't this a joy? Perhaps this sounds to some readers like a contradiction of the model we offer, however, it is very much about working from the inside out. Only when we truly embrace diversity, can we utilise the wide skill bases we have and offer our very best to the young people and families we strive to serve.

Exercise 6.2

Who does what?

Let us now examine the barriers to effective and dynamic management of SEND cases and consider some practical solutions that you could implement within your school. Firstly, we invite you to ask yourself who currently takes responsibility for the planning and input for the children and families in your care/class, either with EHCPs or where you have awareness that there are special educational needs (including psycho-social and welfare) indicated or presenting. If the person responsible is you, who else has a supporting role or is providing interventions? Is it enough, or could the situation be better? The magic wand question: in an ideal world, what level of support would you want for the students and families you are thinking of now? This exercise may take some time, but please make yourselves some notes – about what you would like to see being put in place, in and out of school.

It can be a depressing task, as we are faced with the realities of budgets, lack of resourcing and high thresholds plus waiting lists to access much needed services to support our children and families. However, unless we consider the dream-team around child/family, we shall fail to acknowledge the gaps in provision, and inadvertently take responsibility for roles that cannot possibly be undertaken by teaching staff at schools. This happens so frequently and has a catastrophic impact on teacher stress levels, as well as making families feel unheard and uncared for. Let's look at some case examples, with further guidance. You might use these and create some of your own examples to discuss as a staff group at school. We encourage the use of creativity, strategic planning, delegation, multi-agency working and signposting, in abundance.

Case example A

Multiple SEND needs

'As a family we could not agree at all on the best way forward for our kids. It's complicated. We have one daughter with Cerebral Palsy and she gets very depressed in mainstream settings because it makes her feel disabled … but she is actually very capable to achieve in mainstream school and it would be nice if she could be at the same school as her siblings. Then, her siblings have different struggles as one has Dyslexia and ADHD and the other doesn't have a EHCP but he has something wrong, and he refuses school most days … it's really hard to get him in most mornings.' Ash and Alex, parents to Petra Year 10, Reece Year 8 and Libby Year 6

Responses

In this case there should certainly be a Team Around Family meeting called, with all involved agencies represented. There should be input from Children's Services, CAMHS, relevant supporting charities, and any privately sourced advocates or support agencies, as well as the school safeguarding lead, school SENCO, school nurse representative and any other school staff working directly with the family. Where appropriate, reports can be made available to the meeting in place of representatives being available, such as GP or Psychologist reports. The job of the team is to listen to what the family are telling them about their situation and their needs, and then to offer the family intervention accordingly. The job of the team is also to highlight where there are gaps in the plan. This is the part where teachers should be supported to get creative. You're experts at thinking outside the box, if you are given the breathing space to do so. With all the aforementioned pressures, it's easy to feel reactive and out of control. However, when you look through the context of the magic wand, it provides some structure of thought breaking from the reactive to the proactive mindset. For example: If there is a waiting list way too long to respond to the families needs in appropriate time … what else is out there? (see list of resources). Do you have access to pupil premium funds to pay for a service privately? Are there local charities, or courses available through community education that might be available? Networking, and the sharing of information about local resources is incredibly valuable and often the most cost and time effective way of meeting the special educational needs of your families. Please see the feature box for how to best implement this within your school.

Case example B

Undiagnosed SEND

'My children were never going to be recognised formally as having special needs, but I knew from all we had gone through – domestic violence resulting in a messy divorce, and their dad making contacts so hard for them – that three house moves on, my kids were struggling. I needed the new school to know that they needed extra care – but I wasn't sure they really understood or could really do much to help'. Therese, Mum to Trev Year 7 and Thom Year 9

Responses

We've used this example to illustrate that there are many situations that mean schools may not be directly aware of the challenges their families are facing. There may be a number of reasons why Therese does not feel able to communicate her concerns to school. She may not really know how to explain, who to go to, or if there is any support available. Often, schools will only be finding out about this type of need when an incident of some kind, involving the children, leads to an investigation around a certain behaviour or emotional concern raised in class. In this case, as above, a Team Around Family would be very helpful. It may be that Children's Services would not be involved if safeguarding concerns had already been dealt with. However, there is much that can be provided via multi-agency collaboration. Charities such as Barnardo's and Action for Children have fabulous support available for families, and being able to refer on to such agencies can make all the difference in really allowing pupils to engage with their classroom education.

Making this real in your school

What we really want to see, embedded in the managerial structure and systems within all schools, is that teachers feel supported and resourced in their day-to-day dealings with families. All too often, we have teachers put in the position of taking the burden of responsibilities that are outside and beyond their remit. It's time that we start modelling the self-care that we would like to see in those we teach and care for. Creating a nurturing environment starts when we look after ourselves, and ask that those around us observe the safe boundaries we put in place in order to do so. In this chapter, we shall now help you to set-up and run an in-house training session on 'Safeguarding from the inside-out: A whole school approach'.

Training for teachers in safeguarding and care from the inside-out: A whole school approach

You could run this as a half day CPD and team building exercise, or you could hold three separate sessions using the template provided in a way that works for your team and the time you have. Don't forget that this would be a valid use of group supervision, if you decide to dedicate a session or more to this.

Session 1: Resourcing

a   As a group (or maybe split into several groups depending how many participants), make a list of issues that you see as impacting on your school community. If you find yourself with a long list, perhaps agree on a top ten to work with for these sessions.

b   With the top ten issues before you, pick one of these matters that particularly stands out to you from your own experience, and take some time to reflect on how this issue has impacted on you personally and professionally. Perhaps take some private notes – being careful not to name anybody else who might have been involved in your experience.

c   Now, as a whole group (you may have technology to help you collate feedback), create a resources list for the general purposes of working with families belonging to your school community. Consider short-term, medium-term, and long-term support. Pool together everything from statutory services, to national charities and from small local support groups, to spiritual and religious groups that might be places families can engage with for support. Be sure to collate a list of these to take away with you.

d   Personally and privately reflecting, go back to Point b. Did you feel supported and psychologically safe in managing the issue that you have chosen as standing out to you? Chances are, you did not feel fully supported and psychologically safe, as you are more likely to easily recall events which have left you with some emotional turmoil. If you bring this situation to mind now, what did you need at the time for you to feel supported and psychologically safe in your experience? If you can bullet point your needs, that would be very helpful.

e   In pairs, or small groups, and keeping yourself safe in doing so, discuss your unmet needs using 'I felt' and 'I needed' statements (so as to avoid the cycle of blame and defence). Then, with your team, attempt to problem solve, using a whole school approach, including the wider school community and all the appropriate support organisations specific to the circumstances as described by the teacher.

f   Finally, coming back to the whole group, ask if participants feel better equipped to be supported and psychologically safe from the group session. If people do not, then there is a homework exercise in figuring out what exactly needs to happen in order that teachers feel safer in their dealings with families and the impact of this.

Session 2: Working with mental health and the impact for SEND families

Mental health is a growing issue in society and our young students; many face challenges which aren't fully understood in regard to the psychological consequences of technology, social media and such like. From the limited data we currently have, the research doesn't look good for kids growing up in this digital age. We can't do anything about the boom in the digital world but we can manage and educate as much as possible in ensuring safety.

Mental health is vitally important to the developing child. There is no expectation of teachers to become expert in the field, but it would be beneficial to be able to effectively recognise where there are mental health issues and to be able to have effective strategies in place to support students accordingly. The ideal situation would be to have a specialist mental health professional within each school; however, we know funds don't always allow for this provision. This is why it's so valuable to see what's available in your community that you can refer or signpost onto. There are also various charities which can help, if you can identify a need within the school where you can apply to fund a specific professional or project to be able to respond to these needs. Utilising your PTFA or board of governors to support funding bids around wellbeing and SEND specific provision, is a great way to take some pressure off teaching staff and actively involve parents and families in financially supporting the school through fundraising. Champion roles are another option.

a   Within your group of participants, thinking of themes and issues that you have collectively dealt with in the past year, you can create champion roles, to put out to the wider school staff to see if anybody would like to take a specific lead on any of the identified themes. This would include being able to access training, materials and resources on that specialism. For example, you might have a mental health champion, an LGBTQI+ champion, a Neurodiversity champion and so on.

b   Agree as a group how you would structure this, so that this was an appealing role that does not overburden the one individual, and that there were opportunities for the champions to share their knowledge and expertise to empower the teaching community and parents belonging to your school.

c   With your senior leadership team, agree on how the champions might inform policy and then how you can make policy come alive with a whole school approach. This is definitely a good use of MDT meeting time, in actually creating some interactive sessions as teachers know best how to do! All too often, policy is written and remains in the depths of a file somewhere, or pinned to a notice-board out of sight, and then we wonder why we have problems. The beauty of volunteer champions is that you should attract staff members who have a vested interest in the subject in which they are championing, and as such, bring an enthusiasm and energy to the subject which will inspire others. This should be viewed as an excellent opportunity, so long as it is effectively managed with time boundaries for any work undertaken in these roles.

d   Talk about the limitations of in-house intervention for example, Thrive. As mental health professionals we are trained at working with such interventions to an in-depth and therapeutic level which cannot be expected of teachers. If it is indicated from a parent that their child may be experiencing trauma, whether or not the Thrive scales or school observations are indicative of this, the teacher must know their limits in safe working. Trust your instinct. If there is no clear NHS pathway, or CAMHS waiting lists are too long, or thresholds apparently too high, take it back to the team and revisit the resourcing exercise. Mental health safety is paramount!

e   Finally, take some time to consider the topic of minority stress. What is it, who does it affect, and how might it impact on SEND families? There is such value in talking about this, as families might never directly address the impact of minority stress on their lives and access to education and employment. Only by becoming aware of just how our students, families, colleagues, and wider school community might be impacted by minority stress, can we support and safeguard to the best of our collective ability.

Again, this is about developing a culture where seeking support is actively encouraged; developing a culture of having healthy boundaries within the school, and knowing when outside agencies are needed. It also needs to be emphasised that champions aren't experts, they would just have more local knowledge and active links with specialist services in this area and look at their application within the school.

Session 3: We need to talk about labels

For both parents and schools, the focus on receiving a EHCP for a student through a statement of needs as drawn up by an educational psychologist and psychiatrist, can be as much about receiving a diagnostic label. The value of this label is great, because it comes with funds in order to provide the specialised and advanced level of educational input the young person needs to thrive. However, receiving any such diagnosis and label will always have a deeper psychological impact on parents, families and sometimes the child in question too. As much as parents and teachers want to have a greater insight into the needs and the functioning of the child, it is often a bitter sweet milestone, receiving that label, as it comes with its stigma and the recognition of that child's struggles. Parents and teachers naturally want to rescue the child, and take away these difficulties and hardships for them – and it can be hard to agree on the best way in which to do this, between parents, caregivers, teachers, and any other adults involved in the child's development.

So, for our purposes in working with this predicament, let's take our focus away from the SEND labels, and let's label some of the adult styles of responding to the needs of the child (see Table 6.1). As you go through the list, we ask you to consider if you recognise any of these styles and responses in yourself by responding 0 (not like me) 1 (a bit like me) 2 (quite like me) 3 (like me) 4 (a lot like me) to 5 (just like me) accordingly. You may have parents in mind that you have worked with, that also display certain traits.

Table 6.1 Behavioural response label table

Label	Behaviour	0 1 2 3 4 5
The Helicopter	Hovering over child's life protectively assessing risk, ready to swoop in and save.	
The Lawnmower	Mowing down a path for the child, removing any perceived obstacle or challenge in child's way.	
The Tiger	Energetically striving for success in academia and recognised achievements over free play, leisure and rest.	
The Dolphin	Strives to find a balance between Tiger and Elephant, with opportunities for child to both achieve academically and grow spiritually.	
The Elephant	Focus on emotional security, connection and social relationships. Psychological wellbeing is encouraged above anything else.	
Free-Range	Believe in giving child freedoms in choice, and independence to build confidence, self-reliance and problem-solving skills.	
Attached	Believe in the power of relationship and connectedness to others in nurturing the child's confidence and security in their sense of self.	

For each of these styles there are brilliantly useful qualities whether as teacher or parent; and at the same time, we can see how conflicts occur between adults with a shared interest in supporting the developing child. Table 6.1 can be useful in helping us recognise the positive intent behind some of the typical behaviours we might see or indeed display ourselves. In stressful situations it can be hard to remember that parents and teachers alike want the best outcome for the children. If we can reduce stress levels and responses, and work with the principle that everybody is doing the best that they can within every given moment, it can help us to defuse rather than escalate drama in challenging moments. At this point, it's helpful to reflect on values from Chapter 1 and how they reflect within this exercise.

Conclusion

By the whole nature of SEND, teachers are of course going to have more contacts with families who have a child or children with SEND. Utilising our values based connection model will give you a solid foundation in effective contacts with these families, as well as collaborative work with your teaching colleagues and supporting agencies from outside of your school.

Resources

Student resources

KS1/2

My Awesome Autism by Nikki Saunders
Joey Pigza book series by Jack Gantos
The London Eye Mystery by Siobhan Dowd
Can You See Me? by Libby Scott and Rebecca Westcott

KS3/4

The Spectrum Girl's Survival Guide: How to Grow Up Awesome and Autistic by Siena Castellon
A Kind of Spark by Elle McNicoll

Teacher and parent resources

We have put these resources together, as all of these books might be of interest or value for teachers. However, you may wish to be more selective as to what you put in a parents' lending library.

Communication at the Heart of the School by Rachel Sawford and Ann Miles

The Highly Sensitive Person and *The Highly Sensitive Child* by Elaine N. Aaron

Ten Things Every Child with Autism Wishes You Knew by Ellen Notbohm

Understanding Pathalogical Demand Avoidance Syndrome in Children: A guide for parents, teachers and other professionals by Phil Christie

The SENCO Handbook: Leading provision and practice by Sarah Martin-Denham and Steve Watts

The Autistic Brain by Temple Grandin

The following links are also useful for both teachers and parents:

SEND Passport (www.sendfamilyinstincts.com)

www.facebook.com/inTunePathways (accessed 14 October 2021)

www.facebook.com/groups/autisminclusivity (accessed 14 October 2021)

www.allaboardclub.com (accessed 14 October 2021)

Helpful information about SEND and hearing other peoples' stories (www.sendfamily instincts.com)

7

AGENCY

─────────── Chapter objectives ───────────

- To understand the concepts of agency
- To explore and develop our own sense of agency
- To consider accountability and boundaries
- To understand synergy and circle of influence
- To reflect on how to manage when there are no winners.

Introduction

In this chapter, we will look at ways teachers and schools can enhance a sense of agency, along with looking at what can impact our sense of agency. Let us start by answering the question: What is agency? Here, we refer to agency as the belief or sense of control we have over our actions and their consequences. This is similar to autonomy, which is the right to self govern. These aspects are a fundamental part of our self worth/esteem and confidence. We can all appreciate just how important this is, for all of us, and perhaps particularly so for teachers when we think of the context of working with the expectations of so many families, as well as statutory guidelines and curriculum, school governance, and the many sets of legislation and opinion which might influence the way a teacher performs at work.

You may be wondering as to why a teacher's guide to working with families needs to address personal agency. For relationships to really thrive we need to respond to one another effectively and appropriately alongside managing internal disruption. This not only enhances communication but also supports psychological wellbeing allowing us to be open and receptive, which can only be done through reflective self introspection. It is a process that takes time and needs regular attention for continued growth.

When we introduced this book, it was noted that as a teacher you are a cog in a much bigger machine. This machine can be overwhelming. Here, by putting the focus on the teacher as a key player, we aim to address this imbalance on a psychological level. Whatever job, role or career you choose, we are all cogs within the machine, and how we view the machine and our role in it is what will help in developing our sense of agency. We also must consider how the mechanisms within each school impact the individual. Sometimes these situations are unmanageable and the culture isn't healthy. We hope this book can help build on your psychological resilience, enabling you to make informed decisions, and help you feel that no matter what you are faced with, there are always choices at your disposal.

Exercise 7.1

How's your agency?

Start by reflecting on your current sense of agency. Do you have it? Have you ever had it? If you did what was different then to now, and if you have but didn't previously what was different from then to now? Agency comes down to the belief of freedom and choice. When we are under lots of pressure, it's easy to feel out of control with little choice. Agency and autonomy typically go hand in hand; however, with all the pressures and various demands associated with modern teaching, it can feel that teachers lose that capacity to self govern.

How do we gain agency?

For agency to be truly felt and experienced, it's much more effective if it has to come from a top down approach; and for any teacher to have full agency, the leadership needs to facilitate and promote the development of agency within the staff at the school. Head teachers must ask themselves what is the morale like at their schools, and how psychologically well they and their staff are. The answer to your school's success lies with your staff team, which is why the top of your priorities list has to be teacher and staff wellbeing. A teacher can only have a strong sense of agency when they are psychologically fit. If you are a headteacher, and you've got to this stage of the book and read through the previous chapters, you'll have a heightened understanding of communication and connection. The ideas we explore are valid for any human contact and will apply to your teaching staff too. It's worth using these tools when thinking about your teachers. If your staff are defensive to your feedback, what might be motivating their defences? If you can, communicate directly with that motivation. Let's look at the experience of the staff team at Sky Heights High School, with a case example:

Ms Abel is an enthusiastic and energetic head teacher, and she hopes to inspire the same energy in her staff team. She feels that generally, though, morale is low – and she is sad and curious about that. It's a large school, so she decides to approach the issue with the teaching staff by distributing an e-survey to all teaching staff, asking about their sense of wellbeing, including energy levels and job satisfaction. However, she is disappointed that not many surveys are returned, and those that are, do not give her the information she needs to identify and address the problem. So she decides she must make time with each department and emails to organise a 'working lunch' with each department, whereby a bring and share date for consultation could be facilitated in each department's shared staff room. The teachers immediately feel relief about this, as it not only gives them an opportunity to talk about how they are feeling, but also, with a date in advance for the working lunch, means they can collectively discuss any issues that are impacting on their department as a whole. The dates arrive and Ms Abel goes in prepared – psychologically prepared – and the key thing Ms Abel is armed with is her agency, and the security of knowing that if she really listens to what her staff are telling her, she has the power to facilitate the change that they need in order that they too can experience agency in their roles and with their classes. Ms Abel has had to work hard to reach out to her staff, and to create the opportunity for them to truly connect with her. But once they do, and she then responds by considering how everybody can have their needs met, she has established a fantastic working relationship that will provide a synergy in this collective meeting of hearts and minds.

Synergy

Synergy is distinct from energy, in describing that when two or more agents come together, the sum of what they produce as a collective is greater than the sum of their separate effects. This is not a leadership book, but to optimise the communication with parents and families of the children at your school, teachers need to work from the inside out and all that we have discussed has to be promoted from the top down. Every management decision has to be led by values, beliefs and assumptions that need to be communicated very clearly and that will lead to connection throughout the school. It also has to be authentic, again something we've repeatedly talked about throughout this book. If you are working within your true and authentic values, you will make decisions based on what's right, not on what you think you ought to do.

Exercise 7.2

Agency in leadership

If you are reading this as a head teacher, what is the current state of your own wellbeing, and are you modelling an effective balance of professional/personal wellness? What level of agency do you currently feel and what support is available to you? Leadership can often feel isolating – is there support for head teachers in your area? If you are feeling isolated this can leave you vulnerable to being in a state of stress, which won't optimise your communication. It's worth taking some time to network with other heads in other schools and if such a network doesn't exist, set up your own peer support group, by writing to the head teachers of other schools in your area. You can use the framework for peer supervision, as detailed in Chapter 5, to run such groups.

If you follow the values based connection model to guide you on how you run your school, teachers will work aligned to their values, have a strong sense of community and be psychologically well. Thus, not only will your school work effectively in educating the students, but you'll be facilitating a nurturing and empowering environment that will be safe and supportive to all who are part of this special community.

Accountability

Accountability is directly linked to agency and is a vital component establishing trusting relationships. The way we deal with difficult or uncomfortable situations can make or break connections. So, the way we communicate our accountability also has an impact on our relationships with others. We live in a society where blame culture has become a toxic and predominant feature in how human beings respond when things go wrong. This, coupled with the fear of doing or saying the wrong thing, has made accountability a challenge. When we are faced with a situation which we may not know how to respond to, it can lead us down two different paths: one in which we go into 'over-fix' and compromise our boundaries, the other whereby we go into defensive mode and the shutters come down along with feelings of being unable to respond at all. As has been discussed in the previous chapter, sometimes, due to lack of expert and statutory resources, this can lead us down one of these two roads. However, neither are helpful for dealing effectively with difficult situations or the wellbeing of ourselves, students and families.

Exercise 7.3

Accountability exercise

1 At this point, let's stop and give some time for thoughts on exactly what you are accountable for, within the law, the curriculum and with regard to your own values.
2 Do you have a clear way of communicating to your school – colleagues, students and families – what are you accountable for?
3 What happens when you do not deliver on what you are accountable for?
4 What happens when others around you do not deliver on what they are accountable for?

By considering these questions, we can address the messaging around accountability within which we are operating. Only by addressing this can we seek to change a toxic blame culture and find real solutions.

Boundaries

Accountability leads neatly to boundaries. We have to work within our professional and personal boundaries. This is necessary for agency, as we cannot be confident in our role if we are working beyond our expertise or outside our role as teacher. We are accountable for noticing and doing what we can to bring in outside professionals to work in roles that sit outside of what we are accountable for. For example, teachers may be the first persons to note safeguarding concerns around malnutrition of a pupil. However, once they have reported this, and they are confident the matter has been escalated accordingly, the teacher is not responsible for the dietary monitoring or supervision of that child's eating. In such a case, the NHS would certainly be involved, and perhaps the child's clinical pathway would detail what the school's part might be, thereby marking a clear boundary and delegation of responsibility and accountability, e.g. Can the teacher please continue to note if the child is lethargic and lacking energy in lessons? Can dinner supervisors please be aware of the child at lunchtime and support their eating plan?

Exercise 7.4

Agency reflection

Let's revisit and reflect on your current sense of agency: Do you have it? Have you ever had it? If you did what was different then to now, and if you have but didn't previously what was different from then to now?

It's so important to be able to build autonomy and agency. We unconsciously respond to our bodies and the level of threat we are feeling. When we go into a threat mode, we look at the world and all around it very differently. We can't stop this, we can only listen and respond. What our stress response does is diminish our belief in our ability to cope. Let's pause for a moment and really think about the implications of stress and how we think. Let's stop and consider what happens to our sense of agency when we are under threat, perhaps certain inspections spring to mind! If we are under stress and we have a diminished belief in our ability to cope, how does it impact the way we think, communicate and connect?

Agency is very much tied into our belief about a situation. So, what does it mean to have strong agency, and what does that look like? Agency is the sense of feeling in control, believing in your capabilities and having the capacity to take action. Agency accompanies your education and knowledge with self belief and a proactive mindset. Perhaps, most importantly, agency allows us to combine head and heart, cognitive and emotional intelligence, in connecting with others and enhancing our capacity to grow and learn as a community.

The circle of influence

Let's expand on the notion of a thriving learning community by exploring Covey's circle of influence, with some direct examples of our pupil-teacher-parent triad, as well as considering the wider community. How much we feel in control of a situation will directly influence our emotions, and when we feel out of control, our level of threat will be activated. This will lead to feelings of stress and anxiety which are not conducive to us being in our optimal state for communication. We need to be able to recognise and manage this, it's automatic, so best not to try and control it, but to bring awareness to how we are feeling and have a strategy for management.

The circle of influence is an effective tool to support us when we feel out of control and want to build a proactive mindset. We discussed in the previous chapter the many challenges schools face due to limited statutory services, stringent acceptance criteria or long waiting times. As a teacher, you may have the knowledge and the agency to take action, but the services that are needed and maybe were once there, no longer are. How do we deal with this? Similarly, perhaps a child presents with certain challenges, which from your knowledge and experience you know require a specialist service, and again, this service isn't there or there is a long waiting list and in the meantime you are holding the distress of the child and the parents. To make it worse, it might be that the parents believe you are to blame for the service not being accessed and that you are not doing enough. This type of situation can be a harsh reality in modern teaching. The stress surrounding these scenarios may also take your focus away from what you actually signed up to do as a teacher, in bettering lives through education. This isn't going to change, as long as we are working with human beings, they are always going to bring a variety of complex needs, which will take your time away from the primary focus of teaching. Having an infrastructure in school which supports the teacher through this process is vital for the teacher's wellbeing. And we would argue that the welfare of school staff is paramount; top of the priority list, with no exceptions.

Teachers know what is and isn't available from outside support agencies. The difficulty lies when we know the optimal solution for the child doesn't exist, and this can leave the teacher feeling helpless. As a teacher you are creative and dynamic and so may feel tempted to react and save the situation; or the opposite can also occur, when we become completely closed-off in a defensive way, knowing that our efforts shall be futile. Neither of those responses are helpful. This brings us back to accountability and boundaries.

We can go some way by collaboration with other schools in our local area, and sharing best practice.

However, when we consider creative solutions, we have to remain mindful that we can't rescue the world from itself, nor should we pull the shutters down and turn away from these difficult situations. Having a sense of agency is finding that middle ground with the balance of knowing what we can do ourselves, knowing what's out there in terms of specialist or expert advice, and using what resources and expertise we have access to, supporting the best pathway possible for the children and families we teach. Remembering we are one cog in a large machine, we have to stay focussed on our own area of expertise, whilst remaining in sync with the rest of the machine … we can't work all the parts by ourselves. Reminding ourselves where our influence lies and working to the best of our ability is what we need to be accountable for the part we play and helping us remain within our boundaries.

When there are no winners

This is something that is really important when it comes to addressing our psychological safety. There will be times when you will apply everything you have perfectly and it won't work. These situations are hard and there's no point in shying away from that aspect. It can leave us feeling a sense of self doubt, as well as a sense of hopelessness at times. The point is to be able to recognise when we have done all we can, within our knowledge and boundaries, and it may not be experienced that we've done enough ... perhaps by a parent, a colleague, head or even by ourselves. It happens when we are working with people, we have to work on how we manage this. We have to accept that it won't feel good. The sooner we are able to accept our discomfort and acknowledge we've done all we can with what resources we have, the quicker we can bounce back. This is where effective peer support and effective leadership comes into play. This is a challenging and sometimes painful process and needs to be supported for a quicker bounce back for the individual/s. This is the birthplace of resilience, the ability to cope with these situations and being supported through the process. For us to fully experience agency we must know what we are accountable for, where our boundaries lie, and be permitted to ask for help. It also important we cultivate an environment whereby teachers are comfortable with not knowing the answer. Having that sense of agency is feeling secure with where you are at, in your knowledge base, and where your accountability lies. This again can feel difficult with the level of pressure on the school system to fix all of society's ills. Learn to feel ok with saying 'I don't know, we can't do this, but we know someone who can.' Or, 'We can't deal with this and we don't know who can help, but I can try and find out.' This is where self-awareness is paramount to avoid the tendency to either rescue or become defensive.

Conclusion

In order to develop a strong sense of agency, we recommend utilising all the strategies within this book alongside the values based connection model. When we have a clear sense of what we are responsible for, where we have accountability, and awareness of our boundaries and what is outside of our control, we step into our power. Owning agency will naturally reduce the stress experienced in the demands of modern teaching, and allow for effective relational connections to be made both personally and professionally. If you feel this is an area you need to work on, please see the resource section, as this is a great area to focus on for CPD. When we access our agency, our self-esteem increases, wellbeing improves, and it feels good.

Resources

As this chapter is specifically about teacher agency, we have not included student or parent resources here.

The Big Book of Whole School Wellbeing by Kimberley Evans, Thérèse Hoyle, Frederika Roberts and Bukky Yusuf

Being 10% Braver by Keziah Featherstone and Vivienne Porritt
Teacher Agency: An Ecological Approach by Gert Biesta, Sarah Robinson and Mark Priestley
Dare to Lead by Brene Brown
https://youtu.be/FJH7dt2K_7A This is a guided meditation by Unlock Your Life, titled 'Setting Boundaries – Guided Meditation on Self Respect and Assertiveness'.

References

Covey, S.R. (1999) *7 Habits of Highly Effective Families*. Simon & Schuster.

8

VALUES BASED CONNECTION MODEL

―――――――――――― Chapter objectives ――――――――――――

- To study the values based connection model in action
- To reflect on case examples of the model applied to school life
- To explore personalising the model
- To understand cognitive dissonance
- To examine prioritising psychological wellbeing
- To examine conflict in the context of values based connection model
- To explore community and connections
- To consider the model and themes in action.

Introduction

This chapter takes a different form to the rest of the book, as we look at the values based connection model, and everything we have considered so far, pulling these ideas together and then applying what we've learnt to real life teaching.

The values based connection model is a conceptual framework that unites the concepts explored in the initial chapters of this book, to bring all the ideas together with the teacher as a central point, with the ultimate aim being quality connections within our school communities. We focus on the teacher being central to the many domestic communities, for example, the interplay between home, school and pupil integrated by the teacher. The emphasis is that the teacher collaborates with these to a greater or lesser, more fluid extent. Importantly, the model's intent is supportive of the teacher, as a fluid entity, who evolves and morphs, depending on the context. In essence, the teacher utilises their sense of agency to full effect. It's important to emphasise this is not about putting more responsibility on the teacher, it's about utilising all of your strengths to optimum potential by working through the model.

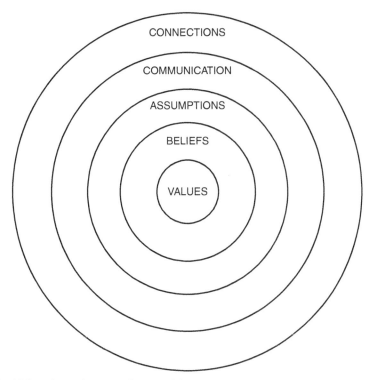

Figure 8.1   Values based connection model

The values based connection model in action

In completing this book, you will have followed a path from examining your own values and beliefs, the assumptions that can be generated from those and how this affects the way in which you communicate and connect with other people. The reason we have the compassion chapter and no compassion section in the model is that it is compassion which allows an effective flow from section to section within the spherical model. Applied well, the model can foster autonomy, as one's sense of autonomy comes from self governing according to our values and beliefs, and when one's actions are in sync with one's values and beliefs. We hope by this point you'll have had the opportunity for plenty of personal reflection and thus have heightened self-awareness as to how your values and beliefs interlock to dictate communication between yourself and others. In the context of this book, the central theme has been to enhance relationships with families of the students whom you are working with. In order to do so, a depth of personal understanding of self is required, along with interwoven compassion. Not only does our depth of personal/self understanding allow us to display authentic communication, it helps us identify our vulnerabilities, to enable us to resource those vulnerabilities effectively, and further enhance psychological wellbeing and skilful communications. It is all of this, together, that makes for meaningful connection with others.

We've fabricated a case example relating to the Ofsted report on sexual abuse in schools circa 2021, and how the model might be used in this scenario. Again, can we remind you that these emotive cases are there to demonstrate our use of the model to calm any internal disruption and optimise psychological safety in even the most challenging situations. We are not trying to tell you how to manage or safeguard as we know your schools already have those systems in place.

Case example A: Alleged sexual assault between pupils

Mr Nowak is head of Year 9, and is called to a discussion with head teacher Mrs Paton and school safeguarding lead Miss Sopha. The parent of Year 9 student Trudy has made a complaint to school and is extremely upset and alleging that his daughter has been sexually assaulted by fellow Year 9 student Ted. The parent claims that Ted has been making sexual advances upon his daughter, against her wishes, and that this has been happening at lunchtimes at school. At this stage, this has not been formally reported to the police as a crime, as Mr Nowak wants the school to investigate, in the first instance. The three teachers meet to discuss this, using the spherical model for guidance.

Mr Nowak's thought process

Values: Mr Nowak identifies as a fair and open-minded man. Integrity, honesty, equality and inclusion are important values for this teacher, and as such he will not make quick judgements, without hearing all sides to a story.

Beliefs: As far as Mr Nowak is aware, there is a romantic relationship between Trudy and Ted – they are known to be girlfriend and boyfriend. Trudy and Ted's relationship and their behaviour has never given school cause for concern … they are good kids, in a typical teen relationship. Sexual assault is a very serious accusation and more information must be sought before appropriate action is taken. Perhaps Trudy's Dad is being over-protective.

Assumptions: applying the model, Mr Nowak can see the danger of his own assumptions. Firstly, he's assumed that because Trudy and Ted are 'good kids' that it's unlikely sexual assault has occurred. Mr Nowak has assumed that Trudy's Dad may be over-reacting, or making a false judgement. Mr Nowak does not want to believe that sexual assaults have happened at any school, let alone the one he works at … how can this have happened, without anybody seeing? How does Trudy's Dad know?

Communication: it is very important in this initial meeting of the three teachers, that they seek to sensitively gather information about this allegation before the process of formal investigation. It is very important that in information gathering, the teachers listen effectively, and act with compassion. Mr Nowak is mindfully aware not to communicate in a style that elicits fear, shame, blame or threat and that in discussion of this topic, sensitivities mean that a calm, compassionate attitude will help them come to the best solutions.

Connection: Mr Nowak has already established a secure working relationship with both the safeguarding lead and head teacher. Mr Nowak trusts that he is part of a professional team that will make good decisions in dealing with this allegation and as much as this is a daunting situation, he knows they'll support one another throughout and do their very best by their pupils and their families.

Mrs Paton's thought process

Values: Mrs Paton identifies as having worked very hard to get to where she is, as head teacher of a school she is extremely proud of. Discipline, effort, perseverance, achievement and respect are core values she holds dear. She always strives to do the right thing by the school she runs, and protect the children within it.

Beliefs: Mrs Paton is a born-again Christian, and believes that sexual behaviour is only ever acceptable within marriage. She is horrified by the idea that anybody would be involved in any kind of sexual act at her school, and believes this to be immoral as well as illegal. She believes that Trudy's father has done exactly the right thing in reporting this misconduct and she has assured him that she shall prioritise this matter with the utmost importance, and feedback to him on how she is managing the situation and safeguarding for the future.

Assumptions: applying the model, Mrs Paton has the self-awareness that this is not about her abhorrent feelings around the nature of the allegation, and that she must deal with this in a professional way. She is able to acknowledge her feelings, so that her own views do not bias or influence the fair management of this situation.

Communication: Mrs Paton has reassured Trudy's father that he has been heard and that she/school are taking this matter very seriously. Now she must also ensure that she hears Trudy and Ted, and makes fair and professional decisions. She must also support her staff team in order that they feel they can remain as efficient and effective in their teaching, whilst managing this welfare matter.

Connection: Mrs Paton has great faith in her safeguarding lead, as she knows her expertise in managing sensitive matters such as this. She also appreciates that Mr Nowak's calm and liberal approach is a great counterbalance for her own rather more stringent and conservative ways. Spending time getting to know the skill sets of all the teachers at school, has reduced the stress of headship for Mrs Paton, as she is well-tuned in with what her team needs to function best both personally and professionally.

Miss Sopha's thought process

Values: Miss Sopha loves her job for the opportunity it gives for families to learn and grow, regardless of the hardships or problems they may face. Authenticity, humility, relationship, accountability and passion are strong motivators and values for Miss Sopha.

Beliefs: Miss Sopha believes that everybody deserves a second chance and that education and inspiration is more important than discipline. With a background of ten years teaching at Young Offenders Institutions, Miss Sopha has learned much from experience, and knows how complex relationship and sex related matters can be, across all age groups. It is her belief that this situation needs a full investigation, starting with sensitively interviewing Trudy and Ted, whom she has no preconceived ideas or judgement about.

Assumptions: Miss Sopha makes various general assumptions, based on her previous experience. She knows it is possible that sexual assaults have occurred with or without intent. She knows that it is also possible no such thing has happened. She assumes that this is not going to be easy for Trudy or Ted to talk about openly, and that this may require further witnesses and for family members to be involved.

Communication: With the assumption that Trudy or Ted may not disclose the truth about the matter, Miss Sopha has to ensure that she communicates enough information to both Trudy and Ted, so that they know how to access help as perpetrator or victim, should they later decide they need to do this privately. Miss Sopha will also need to be very clearly communicating to the families that sexual assault shall not be tolerated, and nor should it ever be in any situation. Communication through education about what is and isn't appropriate behaviour, and being clear about what is sexual assault, is something that needs to be communicated across all parts of the school community.

Connection: Luckily for Miss Sopha, she is not single-handedly responsible for communicating these messages, so important for safeguarding and learning. Through her excellent skills in engaging with families and her close working relationship with the headteacher, as well as the heads of years, SENCO, welfare team and administrative staff, she is able to disseminate information very effectively.

This model does not only function as a working concept for individuals, it's also something that can be used as an organisation. If a school has strong values at its core, that are clearly communicated, and that permeate through everything the school does, there is far less chance for misunderstanding and wrongly made assumptions. This is a proactive way of aligning all communication and actions with your school values, to demonstrate an authentic and value based community. The first example demonstrates how the core values of each character ripple out into their assumptions, and how the staff team connect and honour the qualities of one another to deal with the situation, whilst making successful working relationships with families.

Personalising the model

Each of us are unique individuals, beyond our face is a story, with rich layers of narrative built through years of life. Understanding our own story and how it's shaped us, creates a more authentic way of being, enables us to more effectively respond to challenges and to have an approachable and receptive demeanour which helps all interpersonal relationships.

To effectively develop and build relationships we have to be comfortable with the person we are and have a strong sense of personal identity entwined with meaning and purpose. Through exploring our inner world we set the foundations for building relationships with others, as well as managing our own wellbeing and being able to respond effectively at times when boundaries are breached and/or times of conflict. Teaching authentically with a profound personal understanding of self not only models this way of being to the student, it also increases the effectiveness of teaching all the soft skills to resource children for their next chapter in life and, ultimately, adulthood.

Cognitive dissonance

The problems which can arise from the issues we face on a daily basis but without heightened psychological awareness and working predominantly on autopilot are what we would call cognitive dissonance. Cognitive dissonance is an uncomfortable feeling which arises from conflicting thoughts/beliefs. It's something we can feel and is commonplace. An example might be when you are aware certain expectations conflict with what you believe to be right, however, you act or do something because you may feel your job and income is what you need to prioritise, and not doing so may cause you to feel that this would be under threat. The level of threat which you are experiencing will depend on the strength of the stress response triggered. If we continue with this example, income and job are our source of security, so the idea of losing this will likely trigger a huge stress response. This stress response inhibits our ability to problem solve effectively and not being psychologically minded and carrying on regardless will add to the distress and ultimately cause anxiety. By using the values based connection model you can work with internal conflicts, you can problem solve effectively and have a strategy for working through where the conflict lies. For example, if you're employed at a school whose values aren't aligned with your own, but it's local and convenient and you have good working relationships, this could potentially cause cognitive dissonance. Through the use of the model you have the chance to make a more conscious decision about whether that's a place you want to remain working. With our complex brains we are not always aware of what is going on in our mind, we might feel troubled and can't identify what it is that is causing us stress. This process will heighten that awareness, and help you feel back in control with your choices. Whether that choice is just acceptance or making a big change, our agency alleviates an element of that dissonance.

Prioritising psychological wellbeing

In using the values based connection model, we must also utilise psychological resources to maintain the mental equilibrium and wellbeing of the teacher, such as the balance between effectiveness and efficiency. Teacher wellbeing is something that every school and educational establishment needs as a top priority. People who are well supported and feel their wellbeing is paramount are more likely to align with their values and feel psychologically safe. Without psychological safety, there is room for difficult emotions to interfere with the model and impact connection. When we are aligned with our values we are more likely to assert ourselves in defence of those values as opposed to a defence of oneself.

It has never before been as important as it is now to utilise the value based connection model due to the amount of pressures teachers face post pandemic. When pressure builds we are likely to respond to our sense of threat, as we are biologically inbuilt to defend. This can lead to us fighting our own corner in a state of reactivity, rather than working through with value based goals and ideas. When we are in a state of reactivity our interpersonal connections with others are likely to be compromised; we get stuck in our own assumptions and don't effectively listen. This isn't the optimal state for connection, especially if you are communicating with an individual who is also in a state of threat, e.g. perhaps they feel their parenting is under question, or they feel they've had to fight to get what they believe their child needs. When two states of reactivity come together it's more than likely to be an ineffective transaction.

Conflict in the context of the values based connection model

Parents of children with SEN can often be well used to having to fight for the right support for their child, and they often bring that experience (often negative experience) into their conversations/communications with school staff. This model helps give staff the ability to understand a parent's past experiences to be able to create a productive and effective relationship in the here-and-now and moving forward, which ultimately benefits the child, the family, your school and the teacher … everyone's a winner! When we can recognise that reactivity in someone else, we can keep in check our own emotional distress and really help the individual feel heard. If you can then meet them with compassion, not only have you been able to optimise communication and connection, you are building trust. Trust is something we have only briefly touched on, however, it's a key element to any relationship. When you truly listen and respond in a compassionate way, others will feel safe with you; they will have trust in you and your competence. These are fundamental aspects of quality connections.

This is where the importance of being able to effectively regulate your emotions whilst applying the model is paramount. Without insight and self-awareness, it's easy for our emotions to take over as we slide into our threat response. Once that threat response has been triggered, our brain's reconnaissance for danger is activated, looking for anything that can be seen as a threat and this is what, in psychological terms, is called 'negative bias'. This unconscious bias is convincing and reactive and plays havoc with the assumptions part of our values based connection model. Negative bias comes into play in any situation in which we experience a threat response: our brain is actively looking for the danger, looking for the negative. It's not possible to stop this automatic response, however, using our model will heighten personal awareness, enabling us to effectively regulate our emotions and recognise any negative bias corrupting our perception.

In another scenario, alternatively, there might be no assumptions needed to receive negative messaging. Perhaps the person you are communicating with makes no pretence about how they feel about you or your competence. This is naturally going to stimulate your threat response and this is completely normal. However, what the values based connection model does in this case is allow you to regulate your emotions effectively and hopefully have further insight into why the individual is behaving the way they are. This might enable you to meet them on where things have been impacted, and check-out if this person's values have been compromised, through an assumption or miscommunication. By understanding if and where there has been a blockage of movement within the model, you're going to be more effective at conflict resolution. The more you can keep your emotions as regulated as possible in difficult situations, the more likely you are going to be able to understand and listen to others.

So, let's look at a second case example and how we might use the model to work through. Please remember that these situations are fabricated but chosen to represent real-life challenges.

Case example B: Death of a parent through suicide

Twins Lucille and Hudson are in Year 6 and their younger sibling Brianna is in Year 1 at the same small village primary school. Their Mum, Mrs Beatriz, is a teaching assistant in Foundation at their school. Their Dad had been out of work for some time due to mental health problems. One morning, Mum calls into school to give the tragic news that her husband has completed suicide. Mum wants the children to go to school to have as much 'normality' as possible, but is going to take some time off herself to try and cope best she can. She has no family support outside of their household.

Headteacher Mr Baudin has taken the call and has asked how the family would like this information shared, given that Mrs Beatriz is a staff member and this is a small rural school where most of the families know one another. Mrs Beatriz asked if the staff could all be informed and obviously to be sensitive to the children's emotions during this time.

Mr Baudin manages this, applying the spherical model, with compassion at every stage.

Mr Baudin's thought process

Values: Mr Baudin prides himself on family values which he places at the centre of all school life. Mr Baudin holds high the values of commitment, respect, team spirit, kindness, and charity. He endeavours to treat his staff as he would his siblings, and the students almost like his own children in his regard and care for them.

Beliefs: Mr Baudin believes that as a school, there is no challenge too great for any individual or family belonging to this wonderful community, to overcome. He believes that it takes a village to raise a child, and prides himself in being a key player in the facilitation of this community effort. The loss of a parent from this community is devastating to Mr Baudin, and he fears the impact of this loss for everybody concerned.

Assumptions: Mr Baudin wonders how things had got so bad without anybody knowing and being able to help. He assumes that Mr Beatriz must have been severely depressed, and that things must have been difficult for the Beatriz family for some time. He assumes maybe other staff members are aware of this, as Mrs Beatriz has close friends amongst the other staff and parents within the school. He assumes that others will volunteer to take key support roles for those directly impacted by bereavement and knows that the school counsellor and school chaplain can immediately be deployed, presuming this will be welcomed.

Communications: with awareness of his own assumptions and the many questions and assumptions that the other staff and indeed, pupils, might have, surrounding the death of Mr Beatriz, Mr Baudin quickly gathers a whole staff meeting before the school day begins. He gently breaks the news, with sensitivity, and lets staff know that he shall make himself available for anybody that needs to talk, or needs a breather from their class, so he can cover. He addresses the Year 6 and Year 1 staff to discuss strategies in supporting those pupils.

Connection: Mr Baudin also ensures that the friends and colleagues of the four grieving family members communicate with the Beatriz family and offer their condolences collectively as well as individually. Mr Baudin also contacts Mrs Beatriz and provides contact details for the suicide bereavement charity operating locally, as well as school chaplain and school counsellor – giving Mrs Beatriz the option of support from those avenues. In class, the pupils make cards to give to the Beatriz family, and amongst the staff they decide to make weekly food hampers to take to the family home. Now, more than ever, loving compassionate communication with this family, and in support of one another, is crucial.

Community and connections

The proverb 'it takes a village to raise a child', suggests as a community we all have responsibility for creating an environment that is conducive to safe and healthy development. School is an intrinsic part of a child's life and a central focus within the community. This book recognises that those who go into teaching do not do so to just pass on knowledge, they enter the profession with the goal of having a profound influence on young lives, to enable students to find their unique way by instilling lasting curiosity, and igniting passion and optimism. With both of these case examples, they are highly emotive situations which will create highly emotive responses. When these situations happen, it's natural to want to get it right for those involved. However, it's important that the fear of getting it wrong doesn't interfere with taking the right action. Working within a school community, whilst serving fellow people, you are going to experience situations which will challenge you and sometimes rock you to the core. Not only is it upsetting to hear of these situations, the pressure to respond in the right way will fire off your threat response. This is why it is so important to have a process of working through what these emotions are and being ok with them, but not letting them dictate what your response is. Within the school, you will have policies on ways to respond, which will have been written, taking into account the law and all the other factors which are needed given the situation. However, the policies don't take into account human emotion, the impact it can have on the staff involved and then how this interferes with the process of communication and connection. However, this model aims to support that aspect and if you have a well supported team of staff, they will be able to manage those difficult emotions and respond in a way that is informed and right.

Conclusion

The themes we've explored throughout this book interlock, with the ultimate goal to equip teachers with the confidence to have a 'whatever happens I have the ability to deal with it' attitude, through development of personal understanding to optimise connected and meaningful relationships with the families. However, whilst working with people, we have to consider those occasions when we might follow all the guidance and work with everything we have and it still won't be good enough for some. These situations can haunt and leave an impact that goes on to affect further communications. We have aimed to provide the opportunity for you to recognise and respond to such challenges through development of a structured and rigorous support system within your school, such as peer supervision, to cope with such events.

At challenging times, looking after our own wellbeing can fall down our priority list, and we can lose sight of value based goals. Only by resourcing ourselves can we fully look after the wellbeing of others. In doing so, not only do teachers communicate authentically, but model valuable lessons on taking personal responsibility for self-nurture, demonstrating fair accountability, with an adaptable and flexible attitude. These life lessons are as important in school as they are in our wider education and communities.

The values based connection model's intention is to support teachers, to feel in control, with a heightened sense of agency, enabling you to continue to make significant changes in many lives across your career. Most children and adults can remember at least one teacher who had a profound influence on their life, as authors we can relate that. We feel passionately about that and believe this should be nurtured and honoured.

Ultimately, it is remembering we can't have all the answers to every situation, but with the values based connection model we can meet the problem with curiosity and compassion which will heighten collaboration, strengthen relationships and offer the best possible outcome with the resources we have available. Looking forward, we are moving into a new world post pandemic, a time where all our vulnerabilities have been laid bare with a long road ahead before we have a clear understanding of the impact lockdown has had on everyone, most of all children. It's also a time which should celebrate the resilience and the resourcefulness of teachers. The constant changes that have been faced, having to adapt at a moment's notice, keeping learning as interesting and accessible within the resources you had available. There's no question that the impact of the pandemic has really taken its toll on teachers. We hope this book goes some way to looking at a new perspective of continuing with passion to do amazing things for our future generations.

INDEX